Voices of Women in AA

——————— ✳ ———————

Stories of experience, strength and hope
from Grapevine

Voices
of
Women
in
AA

———————✳———————

Stories of experience, strength and hope
from Grapevine

AAGRAPEVINE,Inc.
New York, New York
WWW. AAGRAPEVINE.ORG

AA Preamble

Alcoholics Anonymous is a fellowship of men and women
who share their experience, strength and hope
with each other that they may solve their common problem
and help others to recover from alcoholism.

The only requirement for membership is a desire to stop drinking.
There are no dues or fees for AA membership;
we are self-supporting through our own contributions.
AA is not allied with any sect, denomination, politics, organization
or institution; does not wish to engage in any controversy,
neither endorses nor opposes any causes.

Our primary purpose is to stay sober
and help other alcoholics to achieve sobriety.

Contents

CHAPTER ONE

Our Beloved Friends

Non-alcoholic women who helped AA early in its history

CHAPTER FIVE

Beyond Her Wildest Dreams

Recovery making powerful changes in the lives of AA women

CHAPTER SIX

Forming True Partnerships

AA women on repairing, renewing and rethinking romantic relationships

CHAPTER SEVEN

Our Families

Sober women heal and grow in their relationships with their children, partners and parents

CHAPTER EIGHT

Worker Among Workers

Sober women in the workplace

CHAPTER NINE

Lifelong Friends

Sober women finding new, often unexpected, friendships

CHAPTER TEN

Women's Meetings

Women find fellowship and recovery together

Welcome

"To watch people recover, to see them help others,
to watch loneliness vanish, to see a fellowship grow
up about you, to have a host of friends—this is an
experience you must not miss."

—Bill W., *Alcoholics Anonymous*

Women have been central to Alcoholics Anonymous from its inception. Many women, not necessarily alcoholic, provided inspiration, direction and support as the foundation of AA was being established. Nevertheless, in the early years, alcoholic women who came to AA seeking help for themselves generally found a Fellowship of men. The stories that these women tell are profiles in courage, as they struggle, and ultimately succeed, in claiming their seats in AA and their sobriety.*

Voices of Women in AA is a collection of 61 stories that were originally published in Grapevine. They are organized into chapters devoted to early AA, spirituality, sponsorship, life changes, relationships, family, careers and friendships. The book concludes with a chapter devoted to women's meetings.*

Chapter One features stories by or about non-alcoholic women who contributed to AA early in its history. Some of their names, such as Lois Wilson, Anne Smith and Henrietta Seiberling, will likely be familiar. Other readers may be encountering these names for the first time.*

Chapter Two puts the reader into the shoes of some of the earliest alcoholic women who came to AA seeking help for themselves. They were pioneers. Their stories leave an important legacy of AA recovery.*

Some of these early struggles can seem like ancient history to us now, since women alcoholics quickly find their seats in the rooms of AA every day. The remaining chapters turn our attention to the* *challenges for AA women in facing "life on life's terms" in sobriety, often involving the very concerns that once fueled their drinking. Here, sober women write about repairing family relationships, healing abuse from the past, building friendships with other sober women, exploring romance, having careers and dreams and pursuing them, and the value of women's meetings.*

In the Big Book, the chapter "A Vision for You" states: "Some day we hope that every alcoholic who journeys will find a fellowship of Alcoholics Anonymous at his destination." Indeed, Voices of Women in AA *chronicles the journeys of alcoholic women who did find the AA Fellowship to have sober, meaningful lives.*

CHAPTER ONE

Our Beloved Friends

———— * ————

Non-alcoholic women who helped AA early in its history

The history of Alcoholics Anonymous includes individuals, non-alcoholics, who made important contributions to the founding of our Fellowship. Some familiar names, such as Dr. Silkworth and columnist Jack Alexander, were men. There were also women. The stories in this chapter are by or about these women, who provided inspiration, direction and support at a time when it was needed.

This chapter opens with a story by someone who remains widely beloved in the Fellowship: Lois Wilson, the wife of our co-founder, Bill W. In the article "Family Circle," Lois uses her own experience as the spouse of a recovering alcoholic to show how she applies AA's Twelve Steps to her own life. There's also a story about Anne Smith, the wife of Dr. Bob, our other co-founder. This Akron woman is another beloved figure in early AA; Anne may well have been the first person to understand "the miracle of what passed between Bill and Dr. Bob."

The story "What We Were Like" is a profile of Akron resident Henrietta Seiberling. It was Henrietta who put Bill W. and Dr. Bob together—and the rest is history. In this story, Bill calls his gratitude to Henrietta "timeless."

In "What a Doctor Learned From AA," published in 1940, Dr. Ruth Fox describes how hearing an AA speaker for the first time turned her into an advocate for our program, well before there was any public recognition for the program

These women had faith that recovery from alcoholism might be possible at a time when nothing else seemed to work.

Family Circle
August 1953

Lois W., AA's "first lady" as the non-alcoholic wife of Bill, the co-founder of Alcoholics Anonymous, tells the story of her own adventure in growth, applying AA principles to her own life.   –The Editors

W e have often heard it said that the Twelve Steps of AA are a way of life for anyone, if you substitute for the word "alcohol" any particular problem of life. For a close relative of an AA, a wife or husband, even the word "alcohol" does not need to be changed in the First Step. Simply leave out "alcoholic" in the last, thus: "carry the message to others, etc."

We wives and husbands of AA in our Family Group try to live by the Twelve Steps, and the following is how one wife applies the Twelve Steps to herself:

Step 1. We admitted we were powerless over alcohol—that our lives had become unmanageable.

I was just as powerless over my husband's alcoholism as he. I tried in every way I knew to control his drinking. My own life was indeed unmanageable. I was forced into doing and being that which I did not want to do or be. And I tried to manage Bill's life as well as my own. I wanted to get inside his brain and turn the screws in what I thought was the right direction. But I finally saw how mistaken I was. I, too, was powerless over alcohol.

Step 2. Came to believe that a Power greater than ourselves could restore us to sanity.

My thinking was distorted, my nerves over-wrought. I held fears and attitudes that certainly were not sane. I finally realized that I had to be restored to sanity also and that only by having faith in God, in AA, in my husband and myself, could this come about.

Step 3. Made a decision to turn our will and our lives over to the care of God as we understood him.

Self-sufficiency and the habit of acting as mother, nurse, caretaker and breadwinner added to the fact of always being considered on the credit side of the ledger, with my husband on the debit side, caused me to have a smug feeling of rightness. At the same time, illogically, I felt a failure at my life's job. All this made me blind for a long time to the fact that I needed to turn my will and my life over to the care of God. Smugness is the very worst sin of all, I do believe. No shaft of light can pierce the armour of self-righteousness.

Step 4. Made a searching and fearless moral inventory of ourselves.

Here is where, when I tried to be really honest, I received a tremendous shock. Many of the things that I thought I did unselfishly were, when I tracked them down, pure rationalizations—rationalizations to get my own way about something. This disclosure doubled my need to live by the 12 Steps as completely as I could.

Step 5. Admitted to God, to ourselves, and to another human being the exact nature of our wrongs.

I found this was just as necessary for me to do as it was for an alcoholic, even more so perhaps, because of my former "mother-and-bad-boy" attitude toward Bill. Admitting my wrongs helped so much to balance our relationship, to bring it closer to the ideal of partnership in marriage.

Step 6. Were entirely ready to have God remove all these defects of character.

I came to realize there were selfish thoughts, feelings and actions that I had felt justified in keeping because of what Bill or someone else had done to me. I had to try very hard to want God to remove these.

There was, for instance, my self-pity at losing Bill's companionship, now that the house was full of drunks, and we saw each other alone so seldom. At that time I didn't realize the importance of his working with other alcoholics. In order to banish his alcoholic obsession he needed to be equally obsessed by AA.

In the early days there was also my deep and unconscious resentment because someone else had done in a few minutes what I had tried my whole married life to do. Now I realize that a wife can rarely if ever do this job. The sick alcoholic feels his wife's account has been written on the credit page of life's ledger. But he knows his own has been on the debit side; therefore she cannot possibly understand. Another alcoholic, with similar debit entry, immediately identifies himself as a non-alcoholic really cannot. This important fact took me a long time to recognize. I could find no peace of mind until I did so.

Step 7. Humbly asked Him to remove our shortcomings.

"Humbly" was a word I never fully understood. Today it means "in proportion," an honest relationship between myself and my fellow man, and myself and God. While striving for humility myself, it was encouraging to see my husband's growth in humility. While he was drinking he was the most inferiority-ridden person in the world. After AA, from a doormat he bounced way up to superiority over everyone else, including me. This was pretty hard to take "after all the good I done him." Of course few wives at first can see how natural it is for the alcoholic to feel that the most wonderful people in the world are AAs living the only true principles. Since I, too, was trying to live the AA program, this was the very point where I had to look to my own humility, regardless of my husband's progress or lack of it.

Step 8. Made a list of all persons we had harmed, and became willing to make amends to them all.

At first I couldn't think of anyone I had harmed. But when I broke through my own smugness even a little, I saw many relatives and friends whom I had resented; I had given short, irritated answers and had even imperiled long-standing friendships. In fact, I remember one friend that I threw a book at when, after a nerve-racking day, he annoyed me. (Throwing seems to have been my pet temper outlet.) I try to keep this list up-to-date. And I also try to shorten it.

Step 9. Made direct amends to such people wherever possible, except when to do so would injure them or others.

This is just as important for me as for the alcoholic. To have serenity and joy in living and doing, to be able to withstand the hard knocks that come along, and to help others do the same, I found I had to make specific amends for each harm done. I couldn't help others while emotionally sick myself.

Step 10. Continued to take personal inventory and when we were wrong promptly admitted it.

It is astounding how each time I take an inventory I find some new rationalization, some new way I have been fooling myself that I hadn't recognized before. It is so easy to fool oneself about motives. And admitting it is so hard, but so beneficial.

Step 11. Sought through prayer and meditation to improve our conscious contact with God as we understood him, praying only for knowledge of His will for us and the power to carry that out.

I am just beginning to understand how to pray. Bargaining with God is not real prayer, and asking him for what I want, even good things, I've had to learn, is not the highest form of prayer. I used to think I knew what was good for me and I, the captain, would give my instructions to my lieutenant, God, to carry out. That is very different from praying only for the knowledge of God's will and the power for me to carry it out.

Time for meditation is hard to find, I imagine, for most of us. Today's living is so involved. But I've set aside a few minutes night and morning. I am filled with gratitude to God these days. It is one of my principal subjects for meditation; gratitude for all the love and beauty and friends around me; gratitude even for the hard days of long ago that taught me so much. At least I've made a start and have improved to some small degree my conscious contact with God.

Step 12. Having had a spiritual awakening as the result of these steps, we tried to carry this message to others, and to practice these principles in all our affairs.

I am like many AAs who do not realize when their spiritual awakening occurred. Mine was a slow developing experience. Even following a sudden spiritual awakening, no one can stand still. One either moves forward, or slips backward. In retrospect, I can see a change for the better between my old and new self, and I hope that tomorrow, next month, next year, I shall continue to see a better new self.

And nothing has done more to move me forward than carrying the AA message to those non-alcoholics who do not yet comprehend and are still in need of the understanding and help of those who have gone before.

Anne Smith
March 21, 1881 — June 1, 1949
June 1950

Somehow we believe Dr. Bob's beloved Anne would prefer this simple tribute beyond all others. It was written by one who knew her well. It came from the bottom of a grateful heart which sensed that extravagant language and trumpeting phrases would serve only to obscure a life that had deep meaning.   *–The Editors*

It is doubtful if now, only one year after her passing, that the true significance of Anne Smith's life can be realized. Certainly it cannot yet be written, for the warmth of her love, and charm of her personality and the strength of her humility are still upon those of us who knew her.

For Anne Smith was far more than a gracious lady. She was one of four people, chosen by a Higher Destiny, to perform a service to mankind. How great this contribution is, only time and an intelligence beyond man's can determine. With Dr. Bob, Lois and Bill, Anne Smith stepped into history, not as a heroine but as one willing to accept God's will and ready to do what needed to be done.

Her kitchen was the battleground and, while Anne poured the black coffee, a battle was fought there which has led to your salvation and mine. It was she, perhaps, who first understood the miracle of what passed between Bill and Dr. Bob. And, in the years to follow, it was she who knew with divine certainty that what had happened in her home would happen in other homes again, again, and yet again.

For Anne understood the simplicity of faith. Perhaps that's why God chose her for us. Perhaps that's why Anne never once thought of herself as a "woman of destiny" but went quietly about her job. Perhaps that's why, when she said to a grief-torn wife, "Come in, my dear, you're with friends now—friends who understand" that fear and loneliness vanished. Perhaps that's why Anne always sat in the rear of the meetings, so she could see the newcomers as they came, timid and doubtful ... and make them welcome.

There's a plaque on the wall of Akron's St. Thomas Hospital dedicated to Anne. It's a fine memorial. But there's a finer one lying alongside the typewriter as this is being written—letters to Dr. Bob from men and women who knew and loved her well. Each tries to put in words what is felt in many hearts. They fail—and that's the tribute beyond price. For real love, divine love, escapes even the poet's pen.

So, in the simplest way we know, and speaking for every AA everywhere, let's just say "Thanks, Dr. Bob, for sharing her with us." We know that she's in a Higher Group now, sitting well to the back, with an eye out for newcomers, greeting the strangers and listening for their names!

What We Were Like (Henrietta Seiberling)
Fragments of AA History
June 1991 [Excerpt]

The following is an excerpt from an article written by Bill W. in the January 1951 Grapevine. It describes Bill's call to Henrietta Seiberling, daughter-in-law of the founder of Goodyear Tire Company. It was she who put him in touch with Dr. Bob that fateful day in May of 1935, which led to the founding of Alcoholics Anonymous. –The Editors

I t was a Saturday in May 1935. An ill-starred business venture had brought me to Akron where it immediately collapsed, leaving me in a precarious state of sobriety. That afternoon I paced the lobby of Akron's Mayflower Hotel. As I peered at the gathering crowd in the bar, I became desperately frightened of a slip. It was the first severe temptation since my New York friend had laid before me what were to become the basic principles of AA, in November 1934. For the next six months I had felt utterly secure in my sobriety. But now there was no security; I felt alone, helpless. In the months before I had worked hard with other alcoholics. Or, rather, I had preached at them in a some-what cocksure fashion. In my false assurance I felt I couldn't fall. But this time it was different. Something had to be done at once.

Glancing at a church directory at the far end of the lobby, I se-lected the name of a clergyman at random. Over the phone I told him of my need to work with another alcoholic. Though I'd had no previous success with any of them I suddenly realized how such work had kept me free from desire. The clergyman gave me a list of ten names. Some of these people, he was sure, would refer me a case in need of help. Almost running to my room, I seized the phone. But my enthusiasm soon ebbed. Not a person in the first nine called could, or would, suggest anything to meet my urgency.

One uncalled name still stood at the head of my list—Henrietta Seiberling. Somehow I couldn't muster courage to lift the phone. But after one more look into the bar downstairs something said to me, "You'd better." To my astonishment a warm Southern voice floated in over the wire. Declaring herself no alcoholic, Henrietta nonetheless insisted that she understood. Would I come to her home at once?

Because she had been enabled to face and transcend other calamities, she certainly did understand mine. She was to become a vital link to those fantastic events which were presently to gather around the birth and development of our AA Society. Of all names the obliging rector had given me, she was the only one who cared enough. I would here like to record our timeless gratitude.

Straightaway, she pictured the plight of Dr. Bob and Anne. Suiting action to her word, she called their house. As Anne answered, Henrietta described me as a sobered alcoholic from New York who, she felt sure, could help Bob. The good doctor had seemingly exhausted all medical and spiritual remedies for his condition. Then Anne replied, "What you say, Henrietta, is terribly interesting. But I am afraid we can't do anything now. Being Mother's Day, my dear boy has just brought in a fine potted plant. The pot is on the table but, alas, Bob is on the floor. Could we try to make it tomorrow?" Henrietta instantly issued a dinner invitation for the following day.

At five o'clock next afternoon, Anne and Dr. Bob stood at Henrietta's door. She discreetly whisked Bob and me off to the library. His words were, "Mighty glad to meet you, Bill. But it happens I can't stay long; five or ten minutes at the outside." I laughed and observed, "Guess you're pretty thirsty, aren't you?" His rejoinder was, "Well, maybe you do understand this drinking business after all." So began a talk which lasted hours.

Sister Mary Ignatia
November 1964

Among the first friends of AA few are so beloved as Sister Mary Ignatia, subject of this moving tribute from an AA who was helped by her years ago. November is Gratitude Month in AA: here is an occasion to remember that the vital strands of spiritual influence, information and help that went into the making of our Fellowship were woven almost entirely by non-alcoholics. Those were the old days, nearly thirty years past. Our earliest friends, young then, are older now; many of them have gone from us. Sister Mary Ignatia this year celebrated her Golden Anniversary as a nun; over 25 years of this life of service to God have been dedicated to the care and recovery of alcoholics and to the carrying of the AA message to uncounted thousands at St. Thomas Hospital, Akron, Ohio.   –Original editor's note

A startlingly large number of AAs, if asked to name the person who had been the greatest help to them in achieving sobriety, would name a non-alcoholic, Sister Mary Ignatia of the Roman Catholic order of the Sisters of Charity of St. Augustine.

How, we ask, could she, who had no experience of alcoholism itself, have had the compassion and complete understanding which she has shown for every tiny facet of the complex mess which the suffering alcoholic always is? The great spirit in her tiny earthly body has lived tirelessly, weaving golden threads of spiritual inspiration from one alcoholic to another, day after day, and year after year, whether her patient happened to be Protestant, Catholic, Jewish or of no religion at all.

Many have literally had body and soul, and early sobriety, held together by the never-ending strands of her love, concern, and dedication to the salvation of people like us. God moves in mysterious ways for all of us, but none of the wondrous mysteries of his grace could compare with the miracle of this tiny nun and her gift to our Fellowship.

Once as she stood contemplating a new alcoholic patient in miserable condition, a representative of the hospital, concerned with earthly practicalities, inquired whether adequate financial provision for the new patient had been made. The response, delivered with asperity, was, "I am interested in souls, not dollars."

On another occasion, she stood looking reflectively out the window and said mostly to herself, "That was a big step I took from music (her early interest) to alcohol." Indeed it was. Yet the greatest symphony of the finest master composer, in its most superb rendition, must seem small by comparison with the miracles in which her great spirit has played a vital part. Imagine a great stage on which might be assembled at one time, the thousands of recovered alcoholics whom she has helped. Then imagine a great auditorium in front of such a stage in which might be gathered the families, relatives, friends and other associates of those on the stage. That spectacle, were it possible, would surpass in beauty the greatest musical production of all time.

Our Lord told his disciples to go forth to preach the gospel and heal the sick. No servant of his has contributed more to the healing of alcoholism than she. Yet in her complete humility we can hear her saying as one of the ancient physicians did, "All I do is bind the wounds. God is the Great Physician."

How does one express in words the gratitude and love so many of us feel toward Sister Mary Ignatia? The answer must be that it isn't possible. Only through what we are and what we do can the reality of this gratitude and love be demonstrated to her.

"Now is eternity; this very moment is eternity." That has been said by her to many of us, over and over again. For those of us who have learned to live one day at a time, often one minute at a time, perhaps this statement has a profound meaning which may not be shared by others. "Each moment of life is a gift from God, which when we are through with it, is deposited exactly as we left it, forever in eternity."

Thanks to her, many of us have tried to improve the quality of deposits in God's eternity, knowing full well that our maximum will be a pitifully small contribution.

Words, even by a master in their use, if we had one, could not express the gratitude and love we have for this great healer of our common disease. Rather, we shall, we must, try to show it through action, in our own lives and in efforts to help others.

Anonymous

What a Doctor Learned From AA (Ruth Fox)
January 1973

From AA members and other alcoholics, I have learned many lessons. Many other physicians who have listened with open minds have learned the same facts. But before I pass those lessons on to you, let me first, in the AA fashion, share my experience—and hopes—with you.

Some years ago, I found out that a member of my husband's family had developed alcoholism, and I was horrified that no branch of medical science seemed able at that time to do much about it. Some of the drying-out misery could be eased occasionally, but no kind of medical treatment produced long-lasting sobriety.

And then, about 33 years ago, I heard my first AA speaker, Marty M. It changed my entire life and I shall always be grateful. I began to devote all my professional energies to helping alcoholics, and I tried to get every alcoholic I saw into AA. I still do.

In the first flush of my enthusiasm, I am sure I made many mistakes—like any AA newcomer, I guess. Often, I found myself carrying the patient, rather than carrying the message of recovery to the patient. But I learned better. And eventually, in order to do a better job with alcoholics, I went back into training and became a psychiatrist and psychoanalyst.

After a few years, I gave up psychoanalysis as a technique for treating alcoholism. I still think it can be useful for some alcoholics, after they have established some stable AA sobriety. But from my own experience, I have seen that simply understanding your problems certainly cannot turn any alcoholic into a social drinker! To quote an alcoholic psychiatrist and psychoanalyst who was once a patient of mine: "One martini, and all your insight goes right out the window!" He had had 17 years of psychoanalysis, but his drinking just kept getting worse.

As time went on, I learned that many alcoholics simply will not go to AA, as AA members know all too well. Moreover, some who go to AA may seem just as sincere as others and may seem to try just as hard as they can, but they do not seem to be able to stay sober. My AA friends tell me they meet alcoholics like this, too.

Pretty soon, I saw that I could probably get most of my patients into AA somehow, and they would recover. But what about those others—those who would not go near AA or seemed unwilling or unable to grasp the AA philosophy? Should I turn them away to die, or keep trying to find something that would help them, at least to some degree?

I decided to keep "pushing" AA as the cornerstone of my treatment, but also to keep on trying to find other kinds of help for the alcoholics unaffected by AA.

Aiming for an open-minded attitude, I began investigating all kinds of treatments for alcoholics. Among those I tried, but discarded, were LSD, hypnotherapy, psychoanalytically-oriented group therapy, megavitamin therapy, and encounter groups. All of these, when properly used by good therapists on properly selected patients, have helped some alcoholics, I know. But for my own practice, better results are achieved otherwise.

Now, supplementing a strongly prescribed big dose of AA, I use primarily counseling, Antabuse, psychodrama, and informational therapy—that is, simply teaching alcoholics facts and removing some of their old misinformation about alcohol and alcoholism.

Four questions I am still asked frequently, and some brief answers, are:

1. What about tranquilizers and sedatives for alcoholics?

Given in a hospital during withdrawal under proper medical safe-guards, these can be useful. But they are highly addictive, and alcoholics need to learn to live without any mood-changing chemicals. I wish all physicians would quit liberally handing out prescriptions of these drugs to almost all patients, and certainly quit prescribing them for alcoholics.

2. What about so-called cures and returns to "normal" drinking?

The alcoholic can no more go back to "normal" drinking than a pickle can go back to being a cucumber. We must not overlook the pharmacological side of alcoholism. Physiologically, the addiction is irreversible, and the condition gets more serious as age progresses.

There have been, in medical history, one or two genuine, well-documented exceptions, just as there have been a few unexplained, spontaneous cures of cancer. But neither the doctor nor the patient is well advised to bank on such an apparent miracle. I have never seen one myself. The alcoholics I have known who went back to drinking wound up in worse shape than ever. None has been able to do "normal" drinking, and the odds must be something like two million to one against it.

But what is so extraordinarily marvelous about "normal" drinking, anyhow? When people have learned to lead full lives without alcohol, cigarettes, or any other drugs, why go back to them?

3. What about Antabuse?

It can be a very useful aid in helping to establish a period of no-drinking for many alcoholics, but not all alcoholics should take it. It certainly is not the whole answer to alcoholism. The sobriety period which Antabuse helps to produce should be used to get a good grasp of AA, in my opinion, and then the Antabuse can be given up.

Incidentally, Antabuse is not a mood-changing drug. It has no physiological effect whatsoever—even if taken for many years—as long as the patient avoids all alcohol in any form.

4. How does AA rank in your opinion now?

It is the very best. I am also very enthusiastic about the Al-Anon Family Groups and Alateen. These two fellowships can do wonderful things that no one else can. Without them, too often those of us trying to help the alcoholic become the "enablers" or the "co-alcoholics," who just make the situation worse without meaning to or knowing it.

I am excited by the prospect of new genetic and biochemical discoveries, as well as the new understanding we are now beginning to have of the brain.

But as far as I can see, it looks to me as if AA has about the rosiest future of all, if you will just keep on carrying your message, with an open mind.

Ruth Fox, MD

An Interview With Nell Wing
June 1994 [Excerpt]

Nell worked at the General Service Office (GSO) of AA from the beginning of 1947 until her retirement in 1982, starting as a receptionist and later becoming secretary of AA World Services, Inc. When the GSO Archives opened in 1975, Nell was the first archivist. She served in this capacity until her retirement in 1982.

Nine years after the Fellowship of Alcoholics Anonymous began in Akron, Ohio, Grapevine magazine published its first issue in June 1944. Three years after that Nell Wing arrived in New York. A young woman in her late 20s, Nell had decided to go to Mexico to pursue a career in sculpture. In the meantime, she wanted a temporary job to earn a little more money for the journey. The agency where she applied for a temporary job told her about an opening at the headquar-

ters office of Alcoholics Anonymous. Nell knew about AA, having read Morris Markey's article "Alcoholics and God" in the September 1939 Liberty magazine, and through other magazine articles in the early 40s, as well.

In 1947, she started working in the office of the Alcoholic Foundation (now the General Service Office), and in 1950 became Bill W.'s secretary. Within a few years, she became close friends with Bill and his wife, Lois, and on weekends she regularly went up to Stepping Stones, their home in Bedford Hills, New York, to help Bill with correspondence or research, or just to keep him and Lois company.

After Bill died in 1971, Nell continued her close association with the General Service Office and with Lois. She organized the AA Archives, and in 1993 published a memoir called Grateful to Have Been There. *Nell never got to Mexico, but she worked for AA for 36 years. At the time of this interview, Nell traveled frequently around the country, speaking to groups about AA history.*

As a bonus to Grapevine readers for this special 50th anniversary issue, two Grapevine staff members—the managing editor and an assistant—interviewed Nell Wing at the Grapevine office in New York and talked about the magazine, Bill W., the early days of AA, and a variety of other things.   –Original editor's note

You've described Grapevine as having an "improbable history." What did you mean?

It's miraculous the Grapevine is still in existence 50 years later. Grapevine doesn't have what a lot of magazines have—like ads or a sales force. It has to stick to its primary purpose and basically that's to ask members to write articles, to share their stories, to feature events happening in their areas, now or in the future. But Grapevine has kept going because there are many, many people who understand and appreciate it. There are always enough members who find it useful and helpful in maintaining sobriety and keep it going. Some even read it long before becoming members of AA.

What was it about Grapevine that Bill W. found so appealing?

He quickly saw it as a means of carrying the message. And since he couldn't connect personally with all groups and areas of AA on a regular basis, he used it as a primary source of sharing and explaining the important issues that he wanted accepted by the Fellowship. Now, it took several years, as we know, before there was a steady and enthusiastic growth of Grapevine readers. But Bill thought that sharing his ideas in print this way was important. It was there—you could read it, you could think about it, you could refer to it later.

That was one of the reasons for writing the Big Book—so the program wouldn't get "garbled" in transmission.

Exactly. If it's in print, it's a matter of record. And the fact is, Bill was perhaps his own worst enemy in trying to get his ideas across. He could pound you into a corner, so to speak, because of his frustration when his ideas were not understood and accepted by the trustees and the membership at large. So Grapevine was an effective way for him to reach people—without the pounding!

Grapevine is now 50 years old, and we're considering what our role for the future will be. Do you have any thoughts about where the Grapevine fits in?

Preserving the experience—to my mind that's what you do in the Grapevine. Grapevine's purpose is similar to the purpose of archives in general: to preserve the past, understand the present, and discuss and predict the future. So many young people are coming in today and they need to know about the history of AA.

What was your first acquaintance with alcoholics or AA?

My dad was a teacher and a justice of the peace in our small town. I learned about alcoholics very early on because the state police would often drag guys over at three in the morning, rapping on our door. And many of these drunks were professional people in our town or nearby towns, and perhaps good friends of my dad's. Occasionally he'd pay their fines for them—when you've been out drinking until 3:00, who has any money left to pay fines with?

I read about AA in the September Liberty magazine—sitting in my college dorm—in 1939. So when I first came to work at AA, I knew about it, and I also knew that a drunk was not always a "Bowery bum."

CHAPTER TWO

Pioneers

————— * —————

Early women alcoholics get sober and help
open doors for more women

T
he women who came to Alcoholics Anonymous in the early
days often wondered if the program would work for them.
After all, the alcoholic women who came to AA for help en-
countered a Fellowship comprised of men.

Marty M., an alcoholic in New York City, who could have been
included in the previous chapter, reflects on her life after 29 years
of sobriety in the article "After 29 Years." And in the story "For Men
Only?" she describes attending her first meeting in 1939. "I was the
only woman alcoholic there," Marty writes. When she saw the book
Alcoholics Anonymous, her first thoughts were, This was a man's
book, entirely about men, obviously written by and for men ... I'd
have to find my own way out after all. But bravely, she claims her
seat. With a year's sobriety, she travels with Bill W. and Lois to Akron, where she makes her first Twelfth Step call, a woman she finds
"drunk in bed."

In "Learning to Fly," Sybil C. of Los Angeles writes how she initially thought AA was a clinic or hospital in New York. Ruth Hock,
Bill W.'s stenographer, sets her straight and suggests that she attend
the one AA meeting in Los Angeles. She warns Sybil that the group
is struggling and "they have no women alcoholics in California."
Fortunately, Sybil goes anyway and her journey in AA begins.

In "Still Active After All These Years," Mary W. comes to her first
meeting in 1960, one of the few women on the San Francisco peninsula. Her first sponsor, who had but six months of sobriety, was the

only other woman there. Mary also had to contend with her hus-
band who "didn't want me to quit, didn't want me to go, but I went
anyway."

These and other stories in this chapter recount the lengths that
early women in AA went to to get and stay sober.

After 29 Years
July 1968

The author's story "Women Suffer Too" was the first women's story in the Big Book.   *–The Editors*

Today, as in April 1939 when I attended my first meeting, the Twelve Steps are to me the heart of the AA program. By the time I gathered up courage to attend a meeting, I had read the Big Book three times. And I had studied several hundred times the pages containing the Twelve Steps and the suggestions on how to use them. They didn't seem easy to me—they didn't even seem simple, in spite of their clarity of language. But I was eager to go to work on all of them, for they seemed to me the key to that which I so desperately needed: assurance that I would be able to stay away from drinking.

In 1968 I feel no different about the Twelve Steps. They did give me what I needed to stay away from drinking. Within a few years I came to realize they had given me far more than that: a glimpse at something I had never known—peace of mind, a sense of being comfortable with myself and with the world in which I lived, and a host of other things which could be summed up as a sense of growth, both emotional and spiritual.

Always, to me, meetings have been important. They renew the inspiration I felt at my first one. They remind me of whence I came, and how near I will always be to that twilight world of drinking. Most of all, they bring me in contact with my friends and introduce me to new ones— in my case, because I travel a lot, all over this country and outside it. The feeling of warmth, of love and understanding, of acceptance and belonging that I get at a meeting is to me one of the great rewards of being in AA. It is a rare thing we have, which the non-alcoholic world rarely experiences. It makes me know how lucky we really are.

In my working life, my personal life, and my spiritual life (which last I owe to AA, for I did not have it before), I find the Twelve Steps a nearly constant guide. I carry them in my wallet. I refer to them—to particular Steps that meet a particular need—with regularity.

The Serenity Prayer runs through my life like a litany; I find myself using it on a vast variety of occasions to meet a vast variety of problems.

Perhaps the greatest thing I have received (and still constantly receive) from AA is the knowledge of where and how to draw the strength and flexibility to meet problems. My life seems made up of problems, but I have learned that I am not unique, that life in general is just that. Problems and strain and stress are the stuff of life in our times, and my AA-given philosophy helps me to accept this and to live with it. Each day is a new one, and I try to meet it that way, as if each day I, too, were fresh and new. The 24-hour plan gave me this outlook, and each day it confirms me in my effort to make it real for myself.

Twenty-nine years later I feel as deeply immersed in AA thinking and the AA way of life as I did at the outset. For me it is increasingly necessary as I grow older. And it is always there for me, just as it has always been since I first found it. For this I daily thank God.

Marty M.
New York, New York

From the AA Grapevine publicaton AA Today
For Men Only?
June 1960

One of AA's first woman members describes her pioneering struggle to gain acceptance of her sex in what was exclusively a man's world of sobriety.   *–The Editors*

When I attended my first AA meeting on April 11, 1939 I was the only woman alcoholic there. And I might not have been there had there not been one before me whose story I had read in the manuscript of a book called *Alcoholics Anonymous*. Some weeks before, my psychiatrist had handed me a red cardboard-covered document, saying flatly that he had about given up hope of being able to help me after nearly a year of intensive treatment in the sanitarium he headed. But, he added, he had just read something that might help, and he wanted me to read it. He said little more, except to remark that this group of *men* (the emphasis is mine) seemed to have discovered a way out of the same trouble I had—drinking.

I took the book in trembling hands and went back to my room with a wild surge of hope lifting me up the stairs three steps at a time. As I read, the hope swelled and sank again and again. My trouble had a name: alcoholism. It was music to my ears. Alcoholism was a disease. Shame, guilt and self-condemnation rolled away like heavy fog, letting light and air into my heart again. I could breathe; I could bear to live. Alcoholism was "an 'allergy' of the body coupled with an obsession of the mind"; there was no known way of reversing the sensitivity of the body to alcohol, therefore an alcoholic could never safely drink again. This was the first reason I had ever heard that made sense to me. I could accept it. I could face a life without drinking, because I had to; there was no choice—my body wouldn't let me. It wasn't just a question of mental aberration after all; I wasn't insane, or hopelessly neurotic; I had a disease. And thousands of other people had it, too. I wasn't the only one; I wasn't so peculiar, so different, so alone beyond the pale. I had a disease! My mind made a song of hope out of those words. Then came the let-down.

This handful of men had found an answer to the "obsession of the mind" that drove them to drink against their own will, against their own desire, against not only their better judgment but against their own good. That answer was God. My hope sank. This was not for me. I couldn't use this answer. I had lost God in my teens. I had outgrown this primitive notion. I was an intellectual, a worldly, widely-traveled, well-educated, once-successful woman. A woman. My hope completely disappeared. This was a man's book, entirely about men, obviously written by and for men, and a particular kind of men at that— religious men. Well, that was that. I wasn't religious, and I wasn't a man. I'd have to find my own way out after all. I was still alone.

And so I argued with the doctor, day after day and week after week, about the God business. Patiently he let me get my arrogant, infantile arguments off my chest. Firmly he would send me back to "read some more," for I was creeping through the book, dragging my feet over each arguable phrase. He had quickly answered my complaint that this was a book for men only by saying simply, "What's so different about women suffering the same illness?" But this had seemed no more satisfactory an answer to me than his careful parrying of my arguments against God. I had consigned myself to outer darkness and there I would stay, alone with my ego and my pride.

Until the day came; the day the crisis in my personal life did exactly what the book had said it would. It raised the bottom to where I precariously hung, and I fell right into God's hands. Gloriously, joyously, ecstatically surrendered to complete faith in a Power greater than myself. I was free. So free that I knew I could walk out my third-story window and keep right on walking. God supported me at a level I had never dreamed was possible, and there was no prison—neither of my own making, nor of the wood and stone that made the sanitarium, nor of gravity itself—that could contain me. I was free!

A vestige of my old suspicions sent me running to the doctor. Was I now completely mad? If so, I liked it. Sanity was never like this; I felt wonderful, happy, radiant, bursting with love and delight. The grass had never been so green, the sky so blue, people so nice and so good. The world was a divinely beautiful place ... I was free. "Perhaps you are," the doctor said, "for I believe you have had an authentic spiritual experience. Hold on to it, and go back and read that book!"

I did, and it seemed a different book. True, it was still obviously by and for men, but it held truth for me and I gobbled it up. For the first time, I read it through to the end. And there I found, among the personal stories, one entitled "A Woman's Story." Thank you, my newly found God. I might have known you would supply everything I needed.

For a while it seemed the book held everything I needed. I was reluctant to meet the people. I was too busy reveling in a state of mind I had never known: a beatific state of pure delight in living. Yet I was really a little afraid—of what these men would be like, of how they would accept me, a woman. Would one other woman be enough? Would she like me and accept me? Would she be there if I went to meet them? Would the reality of flesh and blood spoil my ecstatic dream? Was it a dream?

Weeks passed and the good doctor took matters into his own hands; he made a date for me to meet one of these men and his wife, and to go with them to a meeting in Brooklyn. I was warmly received; first names were the rule, they told me, and Mrs. M.—Sandy—made me feel more than welcome. We had dinner and set off for Brooklyn, to Bill and Lois's brownstone house. The first floor seemed crowded as we entered. I saw many women among the crowd, but no one looked as if they had ever had a drink. It looked like any friendly gathering in any home, with far too many strangers for my taste. I flew upstairs to leave my coat and lingered there. Lois came up and put her arm around my shoulder. "We want you down with us," she said. "You are very welcome." And she looked as if she meant it. I think I have never seen such sheer lovingness shining out of a person—it warmed and comforted me. Lois, a non-alcoholic wife, taught me about love. But that's another story.

I was made welcome, and yet—did I notice just a flicker of uncertainty? Just a slight wariness, a kind of disbelief on the part of these men that I could really be one of them? I did, for some of their questions revealed it. I was the youngest person there, by far. And I was a woman. I was fairly well-dressed, was currently an inmate of a rather expensive private sanitarium (they didn't know I was stony broke, was there on a "scholarship" for free), and was obviously from a "good" background—well-brought-up, well-educated, and apparently meeting the specifications for that old-fashioned label "a lady." These things are not usually associated with drunken women, even in the minds of drunken men. This I knew from my own experience.

So I identified myself, and found myself telling the naked truth about my drinking as I had never been able to do even with my doctor. And I noted the small intake of breath, the widening of eyes, the retreating but still dormant suspicion in some of my questioners. But for enough of them, I made the grade. I was accepted as an authentic alcoholic, and therefore a qualified participant in the meeting. There were a number of non-wives and friends present, for this night was an occasion: the first printed and bound copy of the book *Alcoholics Anonymous* was on display. I knew I was in when I was asked to sign the copy, along with the rest. And I further knew I was in when I found myself talking almost exclusively to the men who were alcoholics. They so surrounded me, and asked so many questions, that I knew I was indeed a rarity—something of an occasion myself.

As soon as I decently could, I asked about the woman whose story was in the book. She was much older than I, with grown children. Her name was Florence. No one seemed to know her except Bill and Lois, for she was in Washington where one of the earliest members of the group, a man named Fitz, was trying to get something started. He was having a very rough time, for all the prospects, including Florence, kept getting drunk. I breathed a prayer of thanks that she had stayed sober long enough to write her story—for me. Bill said that she and Fitz would be coming to New York soon, and I could meet her. There were hopes, Bill said, that the one other group, in Akron, might have a woman member soon—they were working on one. But here in New York I had to face the fact that I was, indeed, alone. Unique. I didn't like it. I had been feeling alone and unique for far too long. At least the men here were like me. Or were they?

I began to understand the faint uncertainty, the wariness, the disbelief. I began to wonder myself if this program would work for women. I could deal with their questions about my rights to the title of alcoholic—I had qualifications to match anyone's—but only time could deal with their unexpressed doubts as to the ability of a woman to live their program successfully. And only time did the job.

The first year was the hardest. I had plenty of prospects but few results. All that long hot summer I went into New York once a week to the meeting, hoping a woman might appear, find me, know that she was not alone and unique, and stay. Florence came, and left, without any real contact being established between us—she did not seem to want to talk. I saw her only once again, sober, and then she died on a drunk.

I found it difficult to convince the older members that I wasn't a freak, the only one of my kind, and to convince the newer men that there was such a thing as a woman alcoholic and that I was one. The newer men often found it difficult to conceal their disgust at the idea, and more than once I heard, "If there's one thing I can't stand, it's to see a woman drunk!" They just couldn't believe that women couldn't help it any more than they could. Most of the men were wonderful, and fully accepted me as one of themselves, but there remained a curious loneliness, nonetheless.

Finally, in October, came Nona, whom I had met when I entered the sanitarium nearly two years before. She came in wholeheartedly, a quiet girl not wanting to be noticed, but she was there. In November I went with Bill and Lois to Akron and called on the woman (drunk in bed) for whom they had had hopes, but I was no more successful than the men had been. I went on to Chicago where Sylvia lived—Sylvia who in October had gone to Cleveland to find AA in the home of an early member, and who had returned to Chicago full of sobriety and zeal to help others. Now there were three of us the country over—but three is a crowd. Three can be neither alone nor unique, and we were all three too different to be the same kind of a freak!

We used to hold long discussions as to why it was so difficult to help women, why they couldn't stay sober, couldn't make this program work. Some of the men thought it was because women were more dishonest than men, less direct. "Sneakier" was a word they used. I had to agree that this fitted most cases and that it made my self-appointed task of getting women into AA almost impossible. But I thought I understood the reasons for this—and I still think they are the reasons that keep many women from success in AA.

We have a double standard in our society. Many things that are acceptable, or at least forgivable, in men, are not in women. Although the high pedestal on which women used to be enthroned is slowly descending to a more realistic level (and most women are duly grateful for this entry into more comfortable realms), it is doing so only in fits and starts, like a balky elevator. There are still areas of behavior that are forbidden to "nice" women, and excessive drinking is one of these. Many men who are themselves alcoholic and because of this have committed every sin the book, are inclined to look down their noses at women who have suffered the same mishaps, and for the same reason. They can't be "nice." Many non-alcoholic wives are inclined to be even more sure of this last statement, and not to want their husbands to associate with such questionable types.

Women know this, of course, and the moment their drinking shows signs of being different, even slightly out of control, they instinctively go for cover, and bend all their effort to concealment. They become masters at deception, at hiding their condition and the cause of it—their bottles. Their opportunities are great if they are housewives, as many of them are. They are alone and in command of their environment for most of their waking hours. By the time their control is completely gone and they are discovered, they have built a pattern of deception that is nothing short of superb. Such a fantastic construction, built so painstakingly for so long, does not fall to pieces easily, and they have trained themselves so well to safeguard and protect it under all circumstances, even helpless drunkenness, that they often cannot relinquish this "protective coloration," even when they finally want to and know that they must if they are to live.

The double standard has created another hazard for the woman seeking help in AA. Men are not supposed to care too much about "what the neighbors say" or "what will Joe think of you," but women most definitely are. Girls are brought up to consider other people's opinions of them, first and foremost. When a woman starts drinking too much, and then uncontrolledly, this becomes a prime bugaboo that haunts her sober moments. Unfortunately, the name Alcoholics Anonymous is frequently all mixed up in her already mixed-up thoughts with the total unacceptability of alcoholism, alcoholics, and everything to do with both, to most of the people she knows and whose opinions of her she has been taught to value above all else. How can she fly in the face of all she holds most dear, and pin this taboo label on herself? Better to hide in the bowels of the earth, or the bottom of a bottle.

Finally, there are the misconceptions of an earlier more prudish day, when only "loose women" were supposed to drink; ergo, women who drank were "loose women," and if they drank badly, they were "lost women." The scarlet letter has hung like a terrible barrier in front of many women who desperately needed what AA had to offer them. And I may add that the scarlet letter has been pinned on many innocent alcoholics—whose only sins (?) were those of alcoholism—by self-righteous or fearful non-alcoholic women—and men, too. Man's inhumanity to man might better read "women's inhumanity to women," particularly in the smaller communities of our enlightened country.

These, I think, are some of the valid reasons why the growth of the number of women in AA was painfully slow at first, and even now is amazingly greater in the big cities than in even their own suburbs, let alone smaller towns. Yet growth there has been, and a commensurate change in attitude both within and outside of AA. For women have recovered and gone back to their own close little societies to talk about it, to teach them to know better, to let their own stories be known in the hope that they might reach into some other room, secluded and well-hidden as their own once was. Women who have embraced AA have found the God-given courage to face their whispering accusers, and to face them down; to hold on to their sobriety and to build from it a good life, open to the most critical inspection; to accept new values that do not give weight to "what the neighbors think—or say"; and to rely on their own conscience in communion with their own God as they understand him, for judgment of their worth.

All this is not easy. I think it must be said that because of cultural and environmental patterns which are beyond her control, it is not yet the same for a woman to have alcoholism as it is for a man. It is much, much more difficult, and the chances of finding help and achieving recovery are undeniably less. Yet there has been improvement over the past 20 years, and I believe that the situation will become progressively better as alcoholism is more widely accepted for the disease that it is, and the unfair stigma gradually disappears. Public acceptance will one day bring about the cultural and environmental changes that are beginning to be evident. The double standard has no place in the realm of illness, and never did have. Once alcoholism is firmly ensconced in that realm, much of the old prejudice against women alcoholics will die a natural death.

But it is a long, slow process. Five years after I came into AA, in the spring of 1944, the several large AA groups in Pittsburgh asked me down to speak at a public meeting. They told me outright that they wanted to show Pittsburgh that there was such a thing as a woman alcoholic, and that she could recover. Still, it was many months after that before they got their first woman member. Groups have written me from all over the country to say that after four and five years of intense activity and growth, they had yet to have a woman member; I have made countless trips and many speeches to show myself and give evidence of the possibility. This was a major reason why I temporarily gave up my doubly precious anonymity (being a woman and therefore vulnerable to scarlet letters and a host of other unpleasant things) when I entered public work in this field. No one was ever happier to resume that protective cloak after two years of both veiled and crass remarks and looks. It takes great faith and plenty of sheer strength to be an avowed woman alcoholic. I am both humbled and proud of my sex as I see the growing numbers who dare—for the sake of all those others still undeclared, still suffering the tortures of the damned, alone.

Things move. During the late 1940s I had many letters from lone woman members, seeking comfort, company and advice on how to find and bring in others. Then in the 1950s I began to be asked to come and speak at luncheons and dinners of just AA women. I thought the corner had been turned, that no one could ever again imagine AA was "for men only." Imagine my shock and horror when in December 1959, 20 years and eight months after my solo landing in AA, a woman member in a great midwestern city I was visiting told me of several AA groups in the city who would not receive women as members—stated flatly that they did not want women in their groups. Several men with us corroborated her story, adding, before I could catch my breath, that it didn't matter so much in a big city like theirs where there were plenty of other groups a woman could go to, but what bothered them was the fact that this was true in many small cities and towns where there was only one group, so that in effect this meant denying AA to women alcoholics.

I could hardly believe my ears, but the people who told me this were not erratic, newly sober alcoholics, but longtime members who know their area well and traverse it frequently. If this is so, in the midwest, it may very well be so in many parts of our vast country, especially in sparsely settled areas with only small towns.

There obviously remains much to be done. After 20 years, women coming into AA are still pioneers. Those who make statistical studies claim that there is only one woman alcoholic for every five-and-a-half men. The records of public outpatient clinics seem to bear out this figure. But there are many physicians in private practice, where a confidence is considered as sacred as in the confessional, who state categorically the women alcoholics outnumber the men in their practice. Certainly in the big cities, one often finds the women outnumbering the men at closed meetings. Is it just that women alcoholics more readily find their way to the anonymity of the big cities? Or are there more of us than even we think?

Once again, only time will tell us. But I hope and pray it won't have to be another 20 years for all those out there alone.

Learning to Fly
February 1992

My name is Sybil, and I'm an alcoholic. I got to this Fellowship in 1941, and I want to just reminisce with you a little bit about the olden days, what I call the covered wagon days.

A couple of weeks ago, my husband asked me if I could recall my last drunk, and I said, "Yes, I can." I was driving along one day, wanting to go home but afraid to because I couldn't face anyone, and I ended up in San Francisco. Now I couldn't go home for sure—it was the next day. What was I going to do? Shaking, sweating, eyes bloodshot, face puffed up, I'd run out of lies, and I thought, If I go home right now it's going to be too late. I can't think of a lie that will wash.

I parked the car and I walked, and I saw this sign, "Sultan Turkish Baths." I decided I could sweat it out there and get myself in shape, but I thought I'd better have something to read. So I stopped at the newsstand and bought a Saturday Evening Post—five cents. It was dated March 1, 1941, and on the cover it said, "Alcoholics Anonymous, by Jack Alexander." I was stunned because I had read about AA in 1939, in the Liberty Magazine, I believe, one little paragraph about an inch big. Even that impressed me and I intended to cut save it but I hadn't. But here it was. So I took the magazine _____, had the Turkish bath, and even though I was just too sick to think, I knew there was hope.

I somehow got the impression that there was an AA hospital or clinic or something, but at the bottom of the article it said if you need help, write to Box such-and-such in New York. I rang the bell for the bath attendant and asked for pencil, paper, envelope and a stamp, and I think I wrote a rather pitiful letter to New York. I said, I am a desperate alcoholic and I'll take the next plane back there and take your cure.

The answer came a few days later, airmail special delivery, from Ruth Hock, God bless her. She was Bill W.'s non-alcoholic stenographer and had been for many years when Bill was on Wall Street. And now she was still working for him and she answered all the mail from that Saturday Evening Post article. She answered my letter and said, "You needn't come back to New York, there's one group in Los Angeles. That's for all of California. It's very small and it has been a struggle for them. They have met in a couple of hotel lobbies but they are now meeting in the Elks Temple every Friday night at 8:30." And she said, "You'll be very welcome, I'm sure. They have no women alcoholics in California."

I seemed to have unbounded faith that it was going to be OK. I got dressed, but I couldn't comb my hair so I tied a turban thing on my head and I poked my hair all up under it, and down I went. When I got to the Elks Temple they directed me into a small dining room, and seated around the table were 10 or 12 men, and a couple of women. I made myself invisible, if that's possible, because they all looked so happy and were laughing and talking. I thought, Well, they're the doctors and the nurses and so forth, and I thought they would be giving me a pill any minute now—the magic pill, the cure-all.

Eventually a man got up and rapped on the table for order. And he said, "This is a regular meeting of Alcoholics Anonymous in California. We are a band of ex-drunks who gather to obtain and maintain our sobriety on an all-time basis with no mental reservations whatsoever." I thought to myself, What an order; I can't go through with it. Well, I didn't have to go through with it that night. I didn't get a chance because he continued with, "But as is our custom before this meeting starts, all you women leave." And these two women that I hadn't even noticed particularly because I was so desperately frightened, they just strolled out into the lobby. I later found out they were the wives—there was no Al-Anon then, and the women were quite used to leaving the meeting and waiting in the lobby; they came back later for coffee and donuts. But I thought this had been cooked up to throw me out. And it worked, because I put my hands over my face and I ran out into the lobby. I lurked around in the ladies' room awhile and then I went into hysterics and I got in my car and I headed for a bar and I got very drunk.

I thought, How exclusive can you get! To kick me out like that. And as I drank and got more livid, I turned to the people beside me at the bar and I said, "I'm a member of Alcoholics Anonymous." And they said, "So what!" Then at 2 p.m., when the bartender was trying to get me out of there, I called Cliff, who's in the book *AA Comes of Age*. Cliff and Dorothy had been taking care of all the Twelfth Step calls for California since the group started in 1939. I was very indignant. I said, "Well, I went down to your group tonight and they threw me out." He said, "Oh no, no, I'm sure they did not do that. Did you tell them you were an alcoholic?" I said, "Of course not. No, they threw me out all right." He said, "Well, we need you, we need you. Please come back. We haven't had a woman alcoholic." When I heard the words "we need you," I thought, Well, I am a good typist and maybe I should volunteer my services. Then I said, "All right, now, I've had about enough of this and I want you to send your AA ambulance." He said, "We don't have any such thing. You go back next Friday night and tell them you're an alcoholic. You'll be as welcome as the flowers in May."

I don't know what I did that week. Probably was drunk and sober and drunk and sober, but I know this: that it was a miracle I ever went back, and thank God I did. But I didn't go back alone. Because during that week my brother Tex came to see me. He came in the house and he picked up the pamphlet Ruth had mailed me from New York, the only one that AA had. It was a thin pamphlet and gave a few basic facts on the Steps, and as he read it he had a pint bottle in his hip pocket, as usual. He was reading and saying, "That's good stuff, Syb. They really know what they're doing there. So you're going Friday, huh?" And I said, "That's right, Tex." So he says, "Well, I'm going with you." He said, "I'll tell you the truth—the reason I want to go there. Those guys that are working for me down on skid row. I can't get a regular crew together." He was a vegetable peddler then, with a truck run around four in the morning, and the winos sometimes didn't show up. He said, "If I can sober them up, I'll make a lot of money. So what I'm going to do is take them all down there and get them all fixed."

So it was with fear and trembling that I looked forward to that Friday night, because Tex pulled up in front of my house in his vegetable truck and standing in the back were 11 winos. I crawled up in the cab of the truck with Tex and down we went to the meeting. There were a few more people there that week, but the full impact of the Saturday Evening Post hadn't hit. But I got to hear the Twelve Steps read, and also the fifth chapter.

At the conclusion of that meeting, Frank R., God bless him—he was my sponsor and so was Cliff—reached over and got a bushel of mail that had come because of the article. Hundreds of letters from alcoholics. He looked at that skinny little crowd there with Tex, and his winos, and me, and about 15 others, and he said, "Well now, we got to get all these drunks down here by next Friday night. So we're going to have to cut this crowd up in sections. And if there's anyone here from Riverside County, come down and get these Twelfth Step calls." Tex went down in front and Frank gave him 40 or 50 of the letters to read and answer from alcoholics who asked for help. Then he said, "Anyone from the beaches?" This guy raised his hand, Curly from Long Beach, and he went down and got 40 or 50 letters. And this went on—Pasadena, Santa Monica, and one guy from Fresno, one from Santa Barbara and so forth, until there was one remaining stack of letters, about a fifth of them.

And he said, "I've been saving this stack up for the last because we now have a woman alcoholic. Her name is Sybil. Come up here, Sybil. I'm putting you in charge of all the women." I had to be honest. I went up there and I said, "Well, I'll probably be drunk next Friday. I always have been." And then I said, "What are you going to do tonight? What are you going to say to me that is going to make it different? So that when I walk out that door tonight during the week that I'm out there by myself I won't get those butterflies and the sweating palms?" I said, "What's going to be different? You got to do something tonight. How can I stay sober for a week? I'd like to be able to go and ring doorbells and bring all those drunks down here. But I haven't read the Big Book." He said, "I know that."

I said, "Truthfully, I haven't read your pamphlet. I haven't felt well enough to read." He said, "I know that. You're not expected to know very much." But he said, "You asked me how you could stay sober until next Friday. Now I'll tell you it's in that Big Book that you haven't read. Somewhere in that Big Book it says that when all other measures fail, working with another alcoholic will save the day. Now I'm going to tell you what to do quite simply. You take this basket of mail and tomorrow morning you start ringing the doorbells, and when the girl answers the door you say to her, 'Did you write this letter asking for help with a drinking problem?' And when she says, 'Well, yes I did,' say, 'Well, I wrote one like that last week and it was answered. I went down there and I looked them over. I didn't find out how they're doing it but they're doing it, and they look good. So if you want to quit drinking as badly as I want to quit drinking, you come with me and we'll find out together.'"

"Oh," I said, "I think I can do that alright." So I took the mail and I went home with it, and I was getting ready the next morning to get in my car and start ringing doorbells, and my brother Tex came over. He said, "I'm going to ride around with you for laughs." Well, it wasn't for laughs. We made all those calls and out of 50 we may have gotten a dozen or more. Some of the letters were from landladies who wanted the guy upstairs not to make so much noise on a Saturday night, and sometimes it turned out the wife had written in for a husband who was an alcoholic, and Tex came in handy there. And some of them were from women who wanted help.

We did take a number of women down and a few men. The meeting grew—and I mean it mushroomed. But here's what happened. Frank had said, "I'm putting you in charge of the women." Well, to me that was like a neon sign that was going on and off, "charge, charge, charge." And I could be real big because Frank and Mort gave me a notebook and they said, "Now you write down all the names of women and then you get them a sponsor. And you have the sponsor report back to you. Then, when you look in your notebook, you will know who you gave the call to. You'll have the report on it. That's a good system." And I took it oh so seriously because I'd go down to the mother group—now we had two, three, 400 people possibly, microphone and everything—and as the 40 or 50 women came in and they were seated, I could think, There's Eva. She called on Bonnie. Bonnie called on so-and-so, and Fran, and yeah, yeah. And it checked out perfectly, beautiful. Then I would tell Frank and Mort it was working fine. They'd say, "That's nice. You're doing a good job."

But one night I went to the mother group and a gal came down the aisle and she had six strangers with her and they hadn't been cleared through me. And I walked up to her and I said, "Where did you get these women? You know what Frank and Mort are going to say about the system." She said, "To hell with the system! I have friends who have a drinking problem same as I do, and they found out that I was getting sober and staying sober. They asked me how I was doing it. I told them I joined AA. They said, 'Can I go with you?' I said, 'Yes.'" She said, "It's as simple as that and anytime anybody wants to come to an AA meeting with me for a drinking problem that's the way it's going to be, and I'll never report to you again."

Well, when she told me that, tears came to my eyes and I couldn't get out of there fast enough. I wanted to run up to Huntington Park and tell my brother Tex all about it. But he wasn't there, and you want to know why? He had been excommunicated. Because he had started a group. The powers that be, the boys downtown, called Tex on the carpet and said, "Tex, fold the group up. Where's your loyalty to the mother group?" He said, "I'm loyal to the mother group. I'm just sick of picking up guys in Long Beach and driving them 35 miles to Los Angeles, so I started a group at the halfway point. Some of my boys are down here tonight. You come out to our group next Friday night and we'll just kind of visit back and forth." And they said, "No, you're excommunicated," and he laughed and laughed and laughed.

About a month later they called him down. They had a committee meeting and they asked, if he decided to fold up the group and he said, "Nope. Doing fine. Got a lot of the boys down here with me tonight and you're welcome to come to my meeting. It's a participation meeting where alcoholics all talk." Well, at the mother group, we had two speakers, Frank and Mort, for two years. So they said, "We thought you'd say that, so we have incorporated Alcoholics Anonymous in California." And they had. Those who are still around down there will tell you. It took us about a year to laugh that one off, until Tex began to visit the mother group and the mother group members began to visit the Hole in the Ground Group—it was called that because they met in the basement.

Tex advised me to resign my job of being in charge of the women. He said, "Tell them you're too busy helping your brother with his group and suggest that they have a secretary of their very own." I did that, but how it hurt. But it had been good for me at the time, because I had no ego. My ego had been smashed for so many years, and it was good to feel that I was wanted and needed and that I had this little job to do. It was good for me at the time and it was good that I gave it up.

Several years later, they called me up and told me to come down and be the executive secretary for the Central Office of Alcoholics Anonymous in Los Angeles, and I was, for 12 glorious years. So you see in AA you turn a new page and it's all new again. I want to be a newcomer—this seniority bit is a lot of baloney. We're all fledglings, learning to fly.

Sybil C.
Los Angeles, California

Early AA: Still Active After All These Years
March 2007

One of the first female AAs on the San Francisco Peninsula shares her story. –The Editors

My sobriety date is March 23, 1960. I was 33 years old when I got sober—a veritable youngster at that time and one of the few women in AA on the San Francisco Peninsula. I worked with a woman, Kay, who had just moved from Iowa and whose husband had three years of sobriety. She wanted me as an excuse to get her husband to go to a meeting because he hadn't been going and she was afraid he was going to get drunk. Kay took me first to an Al-Anon meeting and that was a disaster. I was drunk and they kept telling me that I belonged next door in the AA meeting. Although I'd been a daily drinker for the past five years and sometimes taught Sunday school drunk, I didn't understand why I would need AA. Kay and I would drink together after work and she kept saying that I should go to AA. I kept asking, "What is it? What is AA?" I had never heard of it. She'd just tell me that it was a program and wouldn't tell me anything else.

The first AA meeting that Kay took me to was in San Carlos on a Wednesday night and I was drunk. I stood up and tried to say something and John F. told me to shut up and sit down. I was ready to have a fistfight with him right then and there, but I sensed he wanted something for me rather than something from me, so I listened and thought to myself that I would give this a try. There were very few women on the Peninsula in 1960, but at that meeting there was a woman, Eve, and her husband, Millard, who were both sober. I asked her to be my sponsor. She only had six months, but nobody had a lot of time. Being an alcoholic, I got drunk the next day. On Friday, I called

Kay and Eve every hour in an effort not to drink before the meeting that night. I made it through without taking a drink and that night I met Eve and Millard at the Friday night Palo Alto Group. This group became my home group and I haven't had a drink since.

Being a newcomer, I was very naive. I was sober six months before I knew that people had slips. I just thought that when you came to AA that was it. People would travel on business and nobody knew if they'd come back sober. Sometimes they'd take bets—like one fellow who had to go to New York on business and we didn't know if he'd make it back sober. He did come back sober and he remained sober until he died, which was not that long ago.

The Friday night Palo Alto Group was, and still is, held at the Community Center in Palo Alto. It is one of the oldest meetings in the United States held in the same location. I'm sure there are older meetings, but this meeting holds a record for length of time at the same location.

We didn't name groups the way we do today because there was just one meeting per town. There were only nine meetings a week from Palo Alto up to South San Francisco. About the longest length of sobriety on the Peninsula was three years. There was a man who had gotten sober in 1944 when AA started in Palo Alto, but he drank and wasn't able to get back for many years. I went to meetings all over the Peninsula. I was afraid I was going to miss something if I didn't go, so I went every night. My husband, who was still drinking and didn't want to quit, didn't want me to go, but I went anyway. Later we divorced.

Although I lived on the Peninsula, I had been raised in San Francisco and my parents still lived there. My father was an alcoholic and once I took him to a meeting at the old Alano Club on California Street. We parked at the bottom of the hill and, of course, he'd been drinking. After walking up that very steep hill, we had to climb many stairs up to the meeting. I told him it was being willing to go to any lengths. Of course, he didn't want any part of that and, unfortunately, he never got sober. He ended up in the nuthouse instead, where they put alcoholics in those days, and they gave him shock treatments.

Carrying the message was a big part of everybody's sobriety and we ran an ad in the paper with a phone number for people who were having a drinking problem to call AA. The calls were taken by an answering service and then they'd call one of us. We always had to make sure that the list they had was up-to-date because so many people were in and out of AA. Before I got sober, I would see that ad in the paper and I would hurry up and turn the page because I didn't know about alcoholism. I'd had an uncle who died on skid row in 1937, but everyone called him a wino, not an alcoholic—nobody knew about alcoholism like they do today.

My first International Convention was over the July 4th weekend of 1960 in Long Beach, California, where approximately 5,000 people attended. I was only a few months sober and I was thrilled to go. I've attended every International Convention since then. I met Bill and Lois at that first convention; they were everywhere and many got to meet them and interact with them directly. I bought a souvenir book at the 1960 convention and many of the early AAs signed my book. This included many of the first 100 drunks. After I returned from the convention, I was showing the book to a gentleman at my home group where I was secretary and he asked me if he could take it and read it. I never saw him or the book again.

I saw Marty M. many times in those early years of my sobriety. She would come to San Francisco with a group of alcoholics to meet at the Commerce High School auditorium, where they'd have a panel to answer questions about alcoholism. The alcoholics on the panel were usually former skid row drunks who had recovered in AA. Most people who came in then were low bottom drunks. Sometimes they told the funniest stories and we would laugh until tears ran down our faces. That is one of the things that attracted me to AA in the beginning—the humor and the laughter.

In Toronto, in 1965, the Fellowship was much bigger and Bill and Lois were unable to meet everyone. They were older and no longer had the strength as in the past, but they were still all around. I met Nell Wing at the Montreal Convention in 1985. She was Bill's personal secretary for 42 years and then the non-alcoholic archivist at GSO.

To give you an idea of how the Fellowship has grown, in 2000 at the Minneapolis Convention there were approximately 70,000 people, as compared to 5,000 in 1960.

I visited Lois at Stepping Stones in 1983 when she had just gotten back from India. She was in her 90s then and still going strong. I also visited Nell during that trip and saw her again when she came to San Francisco in the early 1990s, just after she had published her book, *Grateful to Have Been There.*

In 1961, Sonia, who had gotten sober in 1957, moved up from San Diego. Rosa B., the wife of Jimmy B. who wanted "God as you understand Him" in the Big Book, was her sponsor. After she moved up here, she started a women's meeting on Tuesday night. There was a lot of controversy when that meeting started. Step meetings and Big Book meetings were unheard of at that time. I read the Big Book, so I knew about the Steps and practiced them as best I could, but book meetings were a while in getting started. Nothing came easily—there was controversy about anything different.

I've been active in AA my entire sobriety. Currently, I'm secretary of a speaker meeting that meets on Sunday. From the very beginning they encouraged me to stay active and over the past 45 years that's what I've tried to do.

The AA program is life for the alcoholic, and life is better when you stay sober.

Mary W.
Mountain View, California

CHAPTER THREE

Spiritual Journeys

————— * —————

Women alcoholics share their experiences with Step Two

The sober women in this chapter write from different perspectives about their experiences with spirituality.

In the story "Falling Tree," a woman alcoholic is so convinced she is possessed by a demon that she bangs on the door of her childhood church in the middle of the night, demanding an exorcism. Instead, the priest lets her sleep it off next to the altar. She later finds her Higher Power in the rooms of AA.

In "The Transformation," Judith N., an atheist, describes her many spiritual awakenings, including the moment she decided to attend a meeting at a local jail rather than sleep in on a Saturday morning.

Sister M.M. writes in "A Nun's Story" how bargaining with God did not keep her sober. Instead, she needed to hear harsh words from an ex-marine with a battlefield vocabulary. "I do not care what you are," he tells her, "you are nothing but an alcoholic."

A 23-year-old woman on parole for prostitution recounts in "Coming to Believe" how, after leaving the Women's House of Detention in Greenwich Village, New York, she prayed, "20 times a day to a God I didn't believe in" to not start drinking again. Six months later she found that she had lost the desire to drink.

In "Three Lives," an alcoholic lesbian in a convent lives a secret life as she hides her bottles and huge parts of herself. When she finally makes it to AA, she finds peace, sobriety and a spiritual life that's lasted 28 wonderful years.

These women share their joys and struggles with spirituality as they find and live the sober life.

The Transformation
October 2004

"When did you have your spiritual awakening?" a woman asked me at the end of an afternoon meeting in another town. "I'm eight months sober and I don't think I'm ever going to get it."

I had been immersed in the Fellowship for four years and I didn't have an answer. An avowed atheist, I mumbled something cute like, "You'll have to ask someone older than I!" That seemed to give her hope, but it was I who was unsettled by my own evasive answer.

Was a spiritual awakening necessary for lifelong sobriety? If I didn't have one, was I going to drink again? I thought of all the stuff I was involved in—sponsoring a new woman, editing an AA newsletter, going to the jail meeting every Saturday morning, and being the GSR for my home group. Was I just whistling in the dark until the inevitable occurred? My neat little home filled with teenagers who were just beginning to trust their sober mother—were they all at risk if some manifestation of a God didn't happen to me? Was this empathy for other drunks and tolerance for the world in general all part of my mind's big con job to lull me into false security? As our AA carload headed home that night, happy and noisy and loving life without booze, I felt restless.

Among the books we had in the car was *As Bill Sees It*. I checked, and found 16 references under the "Spiritual Awakening" heading, and another 21 listed under "Spiritual Living." I determined to read them all if I had to, in order to find an answer to my question.

The first reading was Bill's account of his white light experience. I gritted my teeth and quickly went on to the second. It seemed to indicate that awakening was an ongoing thing. Could it be? The next one told me that the spiritually awakened person was in a very real sense transformed. I got excited, for if ever a drunk was transformed—from barroom brawler to PTA mother, from people-hater to lover of drunks—it was I.

The fourth entry is forever imprinted in my sober memory. It told the story of a guy who shared his life freely with others, and then said he didn't have the "spiritual angle" yet. It said it was apparent to everyone else present that he had "received a great gift, and that this gift was all out of proportion to anything that may be expected from simple AA participation," and that the rest of the group felt he was reeking with spirituality. He just didn't know it yet!

I didn't have to read on. I now knew about my own spiritual awakening. It was when I took the first new woman to a meeting and when I went to the jail on Saturday morning instead of sleeping in. A spiritual awakening happened as I left the dinner table in a rainstorm to go on a Twelfth Step call and again when I said, "Yes, I'll be your sponsor and we'll go through the book together." It began when immeasurable grace was bestowed on me, and continued as I realized that I could never repay what was given to me by the Fellowship.

A spiritual awakening was happening at that very moment as I sat in the car, letting tears of joy run down my cheeks, unashamed in front of my AA peers. I was certain that untold awakenings were in store for me as I trudged AA's road of Happy Destiny. It's been 30 years since then, and I was oh, so right.

Judith N.
Marysville, Washington

Grapevine Online Exclusive
A Nun's Story
November 2011

I was an alcoholic for the books. I drank, got drunk, had many blackouts and continued to drink. I was filled with anger, resentment, guilt and self-pity. And I continued to drink.

I guess none of this is exceptional to AA folks except for the fact that I am a nun: an alcoholic nun. On my bad days, I asked to God to "get me out of this problem and then I will lay off the booze." In my small mind, I was lying to myself. I would not know this though, until years later when I got sober.

I hit my bottom 34 years ago, and I went through my own unsupervised withdrawal. I shook, sweated and saw spots on the wall, and finally acknowledged that I was beaten by alcohol. I was then sent to a treatment center. I was the only white person in a Native Indian treatment center for skid row alcoholics in Canada.

When I got to the treatment center, the first person I saw was a wake-up call for me. I looked and it was like looking into the mirror. I saw myself in that alcoholic. I readily admitted that I was an alcoholic, powerless over alcohol and that my life had become unmanageable. All I had to do was look at the wreckage of my life. Everything that I had hoped for at that time was not coming to pass. This was all due to my drinking.

I listened to my counselor, who was an ex-marine who had a mouth like an active marine. He spared me nothing. I still remember his words to me "I do not care what you are. You are nothing but an alcoholic." I can laugh at those words now, but at the time I was scared. Scared into sobriety.

I attended the area AA meetings and I found a place where I was welcomed because of my drinking and my desire to stop drinking. There were no recriminations and there was laughter. Something new for an alcoholic. The rooms were filled with a variety of people, all with a common purpose to stay sober. I saw the Twelve Steps on the wall and it hit me that this was a road map to spirituality.

Steps Two and Three were a spiritual thunderbolt for me. I came to believe in a God that I had previously given lip service to when I was drinking. There was no room in my life for God when I was planning my next drunk. I came to believe that if I was able to trust my Higher Power for today, if I put the Twelve Steps into action on a daily basis, I would not drink.

I came to explore a spirituality that would assist me in staying sober and living a better life—a life more in concert with the life that I am publicly professing. Now, 33 years later, I face a new life every day on this journey of mine. I am grateful for my life, the Steps, the meetings, my sober friends, the chance to take the message to others and most of all, my sobriety.

Sister M.M.
Monroe, Michigan

My Place of Hope
December 2009

I'd like to share my Third Step experience. I'm 47 years old and I'm seven months sober. I was raised in a labor camp, a place where migrant farm workers live, surrounded by fields and about five miles from the town of Caldwell, Idaho. I drank my first three beers there when I was 14. By the time I was 15 or 16, I was drinking and driving until the wee hours of the morning with friends. I wanted to die, but I didn't. I quit high school, like most Hispanics I knew did at the time. But my family said I had to do "something," so I got my G.E.D. and went to college.

At college I kept drinking, and proceeded to drink into my 30s. I got a DUI and ended up in jail when I was 31. I remember being sick and drunk, thinking that I had to change. I quit drinking for about three months, then started again. If I got another DUI, I'd end up in prison, but it didn't matter. I drank and drove all the time.

Finally, I landed in AA in August 2006, bruised from falling and beat-up from self-hatred. I knew I needed to stop drinking or I was going to go to prison. I got my first five months sober, ever, with the help of a sponsor who put a lot of care into me. Unfortunately, I relapsed again, even after working on my inventory. I decided I was just going to drink. This was not a good idea, and I ended up back in the rooms again. I stayed sober for 14 months and then relapsed, due to the anger I carried. I only drank one night, and came back into the rooms the next day, sick as a dog.

I asked my sponsor if she'd still work with me and she asked if I was ready. I said, "Yes," and so we started again. This time, for my Third Step, I decided to go back to the labor camp. There is a tree still standing there, where I used to play as a child, making roads and houses around it. I loved using my imagination when I was around 5. I asked my sponsor if she would go with me to witness me say my Third Step Prayer there. I wanted to "return to innocence," to remember that child who used to play with no worries, no problems. She supported the idea, so I drove her over there from Boise and showed her where I grew up, and where the lady who made the best tamales lived. When we got out to walk to the tree, she said it felt peaceful there.

We stood at the tree and both said the Third Step Prayer out loud. I had my left hand on the tree as I prayed. I felt so grounded.

A lot had happened over the years, as I got further and further away from the tree and forgot how to play. I'd experienced a lot of pain and done a lot of things I wasn't proud of. Through it all, that tree was still standing. I went back to say that I wanted to start over fresh, and be committed to a life with no harm to others or myself. I was tired of hurting and tired of anger. I wanted the peace and sobriety my sponsor carried. I wanted to be rooted in AA and give of myself, like that tree is rooted and gives of itself, even in old age. I wanted a new life ... so I surrendered, with the tree as my witness.

Brenda M.
Boise, Idaho

An HP for the Present
July 2007

One of the things I struggled with when I came into AA was relating to the use of the word "God" throughout the Big Book and the Twelve Steps. I was raised Catholic, so there was a God in my life. I had been taught the Lord's Prayer, the Apostle's Creed, and the Hail Mary, so there was prayer in my life, too. But it wasn't working for me.

I wanted what my sponsor had. She told me that I had to pray and surrender my will and my life, daily, over to God. God, a.k.a., a Power Greater than Myself, a Higher Power, God as We Understood Him, Good Orderly Direction, or Group of Drunks. Even with all of these options of God to choose from, I found it very difficult. I am a visual person. I learn visually. I relate to people visually. And I could not visualize any of those things that were being called "God."

When I tried, the God of my childhood kept creeping in. I had a hard time relating to the God of my childhood, a God who said that I was born bad. I had also seen how, throughout history, people had seemed to use that image of God to justify rape, murder, torture and other atrocities. How could I believe in a God who was all-powerful but would let people do horrendous things in his name? And prayer, well, I knew how to say the prayers; I'd memorized them. They had been drilled into me since the first grade. I said them but they didn't mean anything to me. The Lord's Prayer at the end of every meeting meant nothing to me. I got more from holding someone's hand and feeling part of a group made of individuals just like me than I did from saying the prayer.

My sponsor suggested that I try talking to God, so I gave that a shot. But when I talk to someone, I need a picture in my mind of who I'm talking to. The only visualization I came up with was the picture on the cover of my *Children's Book of Bible Stories* that I had received for my First Communion. It was an old man with a long, flowing white beard, white hair, bright blue eyes and a gentle smile. He stood on a cloud with a staff in hand.

As a 40-year-old mother of three teenagers, when I tried to talk to that vision of God, I felt pretty stupid. How was that God going to understand all that was going on in my life today? That was the God of children and children's worries, not the unique, serious, important, life-changing worries and concerns of a single mom three months into recovery.

I knew I needed to get rid of that picture of God and replace it with something truly greater than myself. In my own ego-centered way, the only thing that I could visualize as greater than myself was the whole of the universe. I could manipulate and create a lot of different situations, but I knew I could not create the universe and all that was in it. Following that train of thought, if the universe was the only thing greater than me, and there was some unknown presence out there that created the universe, then that unknown presence had to be greater than myself. Also, that unknown presence had to have started with a plan, and had to be pretty smart to make it work. I thought, OK, good. Now I have my "adult" vision of a "God" that I can work with.

There was only one problem. Whenever I said the Lord's Prayer, or used the word "God" in Big Book prayers such as the Third Step Prayer, the God of my childhood popped back into my brain, and the rest of the prayer became childish and meaningless.

So, being a writer, I decided to rewrite the Lord's Prayer so that I could better relate to it. It said in part: "Creator of the Universe, the Unknowable, the All-Powerful Being, let me do thy will in my life, as decreed by your knowledge. Just for today, give me strength and remove my defects."

My relationship with my Higher Power has grown and matured from that vision of the old, blue-eyed man in white, standing on a cloud, staff in hand. I have a relationship with a Higher Power today because of the suggestions that I followed, whether I thought they were working or not, and the quiet time I spent every day putting in the effort to understand what God meant to me. Today, I am able to talk with God, not just to God. I am able to walk through situations and feelings that, a year ago, I would have drunk over. Today, I can let myself relax and know that I am safe—I do not have to control everything and everyone around me.

My relationship with God continues to deepen, grow and mature each time I ask for guidance and surrender my life into God's capable care, knowing, without a doubt, that I am safe and protected.

Andrea J.
Ypsilanti, Michigan

Coming to Believe
October 2005

I couldn't believe my ears when the judge said, "One to three, indefinite," back in 1967, in that Centre Street court of New York City. He was a Jewish judge, looking down in disgust at a young Jewish alcoholic. "Young lady, you are a disgrace to yourself and your family. Maybe a little time to think about your behavior will clarify the way life works and your responsibility in it."

I was devastated. At the time, the old Women's House of Detention in Greenwich Village was up and running, cockroaches and rats courtesy of the city of New York. It was a wild and woolly place, smelly, violent, not a fun place to wind up in, even drunk. I knew after I went through the proverbial body search and showers, I would be in for a period of sweats, pukes, shakes and all the fun stuff you go through when you don't get your daily dose of booze. In short order, I was put on a bus to Bedford Hills reformatory.

In 1967, there was no AA meeting in the reformatory part of the prison in Westfield. You made do with whatever you could find in the library. The only visitors you had access to were either a rabbi or a minister. If you happened to be an atheist, you were out of luck. Desperate for some intelligent conversation, I attended a few services. But you couldn't smoke in the service, and I felt more uncomfortable in the "presence of God" than with my atheism!

Without any kind of guidance or knowledge of AA, I began a journey of self that involved a written inventory of what I had become up to that point. Liar, thief, whore, glutton for punishment. Jaded. So very jaded and hopeless. By the time I left Westfield on parole for prostitution, of all things, I felt like a very old 80-year-old in a 23-year-old body.

One of the conditions of parole was attending AA meetings. At that time, there were not many AA groups for young people. To add insult to injury, there was literally nothing for Jewish atheists, and especially those with limited four-letter vocabularies. You see, among other things, I had forgotten how to speak English. Pretty much for the first year or so, I kept my mouth shut. I felt like a complete fool. I heard folks share all kinds of things at meetings. I went to lots and lots of meetings; I had no place else to go. My social skills at that time were pitiful; I had no idea how to develop friendships and relationships, other than the sexual kind. And I was not up to giving anything away when I had made such a nice living with it before AA! I just got caught; that was all.

I was fortunate, or shall I say, providence struck. At my very first meeting at the Murray Hill Group, I heard a wonderful share by an ex-con who had done time at Bedford. This poor, unsuspecting lady became my sponsor immediately. She tried her very best to give me what she had, but I just wasn't ready. I was so indignant that at the ripe old age of 23 I no longer had alcohol as an option in my life, and so very resentful about where my life had ended up, that I decided I'd fix you all. I'd get drunk at you! I did not want to believe I was an alcoholic. I spent the first three years trying to prove I was not an alcoholic.

Then, through no fault of mine, I got sober. Or rather, I stopped drinking one day. It was not planned, it was not intentional. It just happened. Three and a half years after that last drink, I woke up one morning and decided I'd had enough. I looked around for some excuse to drink. I could not find one. So I found a young man who was more alcoholic than myself, involved him in my life, got angry with him when he drank, expecting me to care for him, and decided I would just have to show him a thing or two. I got drunk at him. That experience lasted about a week. I went up to the hospital, stayed there long enough to get the stuff out of my system, went back to my job, crawled very inconspicuously back to my home group, and hid out in a corner.

It was one of the most painful and ego-smashing times I ever experienced in my life. I prayed 20 times a day to a God I didn't believe in to please keep the first drink from jumping down my throat. "Please, God, if you are there, do not let me do it to myself again." After six months of believing I would never be able to stay sober again, I finally lost the obsession to drink. After one year of not drinking, I left New York for California. I was staying sober on fear alone. I moved to West Hollywood, cut down on meetings, but did not drink. I eventually picked up on meeting attendance and after seven years in the Los Angeles area, found what was to become my second home in the east San Francisco Valley. I stayed there for about eight years until I moved to Arizona.

It took me approximately 19 to 20 years to stop fighting God and to surrender. I have not had to go back to the streets, I have cleaned up the mouth, I have learned how to have relationships and I have found a new friend in God.

Lots of other really great and really horrible things have happened in these last 24 years of sobriety. I have managed to get through divorces, college, jobs, business and bankruptcies. But nothing can come close to the life-shattering experience of coming to believe in a power greater than myself that I choose to call God. It has changed my entire view. It has also made my life a heck of a lot easier. It hasn't stopped things I don't like from happening, but it has made everything easier to accept and life more palatable during those incredibly rocky times.

Sometimes, looking back today at where I have come from, I can't even recognize the person I was when I arrived. All I can say is, thank you, God, for bringing me to AA, and thank you, AA, for bringing me to God.

Ann S.
San Marcos, California

Grapevine Online Exclusive
Three Lives
September 2014

In the mid-1950s there was a television program called "I Led Three Lives." The central character was a U.S. citizen, member of the Communist Party, and a counterspy for the FBI. His life was spent keeping these three lives a secret from each other. His family and members of his church never knew about these hidden lives. The weekly drama centered on the challenge of navigating among these three worlds and not getting found out.

I mention this show because I too came to know the strain of keeping three lives going at once: I was a Catholic nun, an acting-out lesbian, and an alcoholic. Drinking became for me the only thing that helped maintain some semblance of sanity in my insane world.

I left home when I was 17 and entered the convent, convinced that God was calling me to be a Catholic nun. As I found out in Alcoholics Anonymous, "alcohol is no respecter of ... social standing or intelligence." At first, I drank wine only on holidays or holy days. Loved those days and looked forward to them!

Then at the invitation of an Irish pastor, I was introduced to Scotch. That set me on the path of daily drinking, blackouts and futile attempts to control my drinking and hangovers. To keep up the image of being a "good nun," I stuffed my feelings of anger, rage, fear and loneliness and pretended that all was fine in God's world. Well, it wasn't, and I certainly wasn't. And I hoped no one would find out.

My drinking career took off and lasted for the entire 22 years I spent in the convent. As I drank more and more, any semblance of spiritual growth vanished. I hid my bottles of Scotch, stole money from the community to buy it and taught others about a God I neither knew nor believed in.

I was spiritually, mentally and emotionally lost and tried to keep all of this a secret from everyone—especially from myself. My exterior Catholic nun life and my secret alcoholic life were two paths that I tried mightily to keep separate.

And then there was the third life I led, too. The Big Book says, "... our sex powers were God-given and therefore good, neither to be used lightly or selfishly nor to be despised and loathed." Well, I loathed the fact that I was lesbian. Something was dreadfully wrong, sinful. I was psychologically sick, I thought. So, in addition to maintaining my outer life as a Catholic nun, and my progressively worsening alcoholism, I was also acting out sexually with other women and trying to hide this behavior from others and strangely from myself. It didn't work.

The three lives eventually exploded into a series of life-changing experiences. It began when I took an honest look at the lie my life had become as a nun. That life ended when I made the decision, with the guidance of a wise mentor, to leave my community and close the door on the fraudulent life I had been living.

Within a year of that decision, I began going to Alcoholics Anonymous. I wanted nothing to do with the whole "God thing." I just thought that AA would help me to figure out how to drink without experiencing the problems brought on by drinking. I didn't see the insanity of that thought.

Friends, sponsors and professionals helped me to wade through the self-hatred, guilt and ignorance brought on by my own homophobia. I have come to know and experience the truth that relationships, sexuality and spirituality are intimately connected.

Thanks to AA and the Twelve Steps I live one life today—a sober life without alcohol. I have been living this one life for 28 years. I have a mature relationship, and a spiritual life that I did not find in the convent nor in alcohol, but did discover here. Alcoholism is my spiritual path and the Twelve Steps are the ones I take one day at a time as I walk that path. No more fear of being found out; just gratitude for being found at last.

V.O.

Phoenix, Arizona

Grapevine Online Exclusive

Falling Tree
May 2012

The Fellowship and program of Alcoholics Anonymous has truly performed miracles in my life. Today, the state trusts me with the care of approximately 100 sixth graders on a daily basis. This does not include the other 300 middle school students that fill the hallways of the school where I teach. This is the same state that has put me in jail twice on account of DUIs and took away my driver's license for 18 months. When I think about my times drinking, I am amazed that anybody would trust me with the care of just one child, never mind hundreds. It is through AA that I have become a responsible, educated adult who aspires to inform and enrich the lives of every child and adult I come into contact with today.

Instead of giving you a tedious drunkalog of my experiences while I was "out there," I would rather share my experience with the spiritual side of the program. I am certain that you—a fellow alcoholic—already know the details of my drinking career and the "incomprehensible demoralization" that my actions and attitudes while in active addiction brought me. What I believe has restored me to sanity is the fact that I am able to maintain my spiritual condition on a daily basis through the tools that AA has given me.

It is through these tools that I have made contact with a Higher Power of my understanding; one whom I choose to call God. For a self-proclaimed semi-agnostic, semi-atheist such as myself, the discovery of this Higher Power was a real challenge, as it is to many who walk through our doors. I believe I would have found salvation in the program earlier had I not balked at the mention of the word "God" in the Twelve Steps, and had I chosen to listen and learn rather than look away with disgust at what I initially thought was a quasi-religious organization.

I had drawn the conclusion long ago that there were only a handful of people capable of having spiritual experiences: prophets, saints, children and virgins. As you can imagine, I felt that I outgrew the chance of ever being in any of these categories, especially as my disease took hold of my life. My religious education taught me that "good girls" don't have sex until marriage, "bad girls" go to hell, and the rest float around in Purgatory waiting for their chance to enter the gates of heaven. I maintained my "good girl" status until college, where I lost my virginity at the age of 18.

To say the least, my first sexual experience was anything but mind-blowing, and the realization that I was no longer pure made me loath myself. As you can imagine, these feelings of self-hate and worthlessness, coupled with alcohol and low self-esteem, resulted in a very unhappy, miserable young woman. I practically failed out of college and attempted suicide once, which ended me up in short-term treatment.

I felt so ashamed of the things I did drunk that at one point I came to the conclusion that I must be possessed with a demon. I had to blame somebody other than myself, and I had already pointed the finger at everybody else in my life. One night, in a drunken stupor, I banged on the doors of my church until the priest of my childhood let me into the sanctuary. I begged him to perform an exorcism to drive out the demons that were making me drink and behave the way I did. Instead, the priest let me sleep off my condition beside the altar, where I insisted I be allowed to lay so that I could be close to God. He also called my parents to let them know what condition I was in. I thank that priest to this day for allowing me to sleep in the church and not drive home inebriated.

When I came into AA and saw the word "God" in the Steps, I immediately had my doubts about the effectiveness of the program. I did believe in a God much the same way Bill W. described his initial belief; I had no doubt there was a power driving the universe, but I did not believe that this omnipotent power concerned itself with the daily lives of humans. However, I was so beaten down by alcohol that I was willing to give anything a try. I was lucky to find a sponsor who came in sharing the same beliefs I did, so she and I had many talks about finding a Higher Power. She assured me that the power of prayer—whether I believed in God or not—would help keep me sober. She was right.

In my spiritual enlightenment, I have not had a Burning Bush experience, but I did have a Falling Tree. One summer day, when I was really struggling with my sobriety and worrying about finding a job, I ventured into my neighbor's backyard and sat on a bench he had built facing some nearby woods. I opened myself to God, as I understood him, and begged for his guidance. I also begged him to remove my desire to drink. Three days later, I walked back to the bench to find that a giant pine tree had fallen across it. We had not had any severe weather, and no other trees appeared to be affected by possible high winds or other weather phenomena. This seemingly healthy, large tree had fallen for reasons unbeknownst to me and landed directly on top of the bench where I prayed.

I was insulted and immediately called my sponsor. I felt that I had been given the middle finger from the heavens. When I told her about the incident, she calmly said, "Don't look at it as God showing you that he doesn't care. Look at it as God kept that tree from falling until you were no longer sitting there." Her reply left me with little room for argument and made me realize too, that sometimes the way we look at things can affect the way they make us feel.

To the newcomer who may be struggling with the spiritual side of the program, I share this advice: Do not let the word "God" scare you away from Alcoholics Anonymous. If you stick around long enough, miracles will happen in your life that will leave you with little room for doubt that there is indeed a power out there, greater than yourself, that will keep you sober. And the beautiful thing about it? You don't have to be a saint for it to work for you!

Anonymous

CHAPTER FOUR

Sponsoring Others

———— * ————

The special one-on-one bond of women sharing their
experience (and time)

I n the following chapter, AA women write about their experiences working with a sponsor and helping other women through sponsorship.

In the story "OK for This Day," Kate K.'s sponsor is the wife of a soldier in Iraq. The sponsor occupies her worried mind with AA service. "When you get sober," she tells Kate, "life isn't going to be OK—but as long as you don't drink, you will be."

In "Every Second Counts," Mindy S. wrestles with anger and acceptance when her beloved sponsee informs her that she has decided to work with someone else. Mindy finds more than acceptance when more is, literally, revealed.

In "Portrait in Blue," Chaula writes about her sponsor being "a remarkable listener." Susan K., in the story "Not My Choice," is convinced that she, a self-described cursing biker babe, will never be happy with a sponsor who seems to her to be a prim schoolteacher sponsor wearing matching accessories. However, now that her sponsor is gone, the author writes: "She is always with me, wherever I go."

OK for This Day
April 2010

At my first meeting of Alcoholics Anonymous, I peered up at the Twelve Steps banner on the wall and nearly burst into tears at the sight of one word—"unmanageable." That word seemed to sum up my entire existence. My life had gone from one I was capably and competently breezing through, to one where thoughts and cravings for booze haunted me mercilessly, night and day—all in fewer than six months.

And now I was pregnant.

I could barely make it through each day without ending up drunk, but that was all I could do in that day. How would I ever manage a difficult pregnancy and eventually a brand-new baby?

But the woman sitting at the front of the room was my first and most vital lesson on how it could be done—by living life one day at a time and continuing to do "the next right thing" when life got rough. Donna B.'s husband was stationed in an extremely dangerous area of Iraq. "I buried him every day in my mind," she told me later. But she managed to raise three terrifically rambunctious kids and keep this meeting alive for anyone who needed it, three days a week—all the while simply waiting for her husband's next call, whenever it would come, to know he was still alive.

She became my first sponsor, and I followed her every step during my first year in the program. I rarely left her side and she helped me work the Steps for the first time.

Donna never told me how to live my life without alcohol—she just showed me that she could live hers that way. She told me during difficult times, "When you get sober, life isn't going to be OK—but as long as you don't drink, you will be."

Truer words were never spoken. I sobered up just in time to face a terribly colicky baby, severe postpartum depression, and the discovery that my six-year marriage, rock-solid through so many of my husband's military deployments, now consisted of a hollow relationship that was devoid of any emotional intimacy or caring. Desperately I tried every imaginable remedy for us, and eventually learned another lesson, all on my own: I could not change someone else.

So I changed myself—my life and sobriety were both in danger by the time of our final split, and that night I took my 13-month-old daughter to a meeting where I vaguely knew some of the old-timers. There I sobbed out my story, ending with the fearful realization that I had no idea where I was going to live or how I would even get my daughter's crib there in a few short days.

But by the end of the meeting, that group of gentlemen had an apartment, a rental truck and a moving date all arranged for me. I could hardly believe it—how could these people give so much caring and support to a virtual stranger? The answer was through the miracles of my Higher Power and Alcoholics Anonymous.

Today life is not always OK—in fact, sometimes being a single parent makes me wonder if any part of life will reach "OK" again. However, through this program, I am now close friends and neighbors with many of those old-timers, and I know that I can count on them when going any further by myself seems unmanageable again. In fact, I even sit in Donna's chair at that original meeting, now my home group, three days a week. We frequently have First Step meetings for newcomers, and I always tell them what Donna told me: For today, because I am here, I am OK.

Kate K.
Lakewood, Washington

Grapevine Online Exclusive

Portrait in Blue

November 2014

I f I can hold on to a visual detail to remember my sponsor's face it will be the blue of her eyes. It was a blue that deepened when it reflected any blue in her clothing or her surroundings. These eyes were the kind of blue I have seen in Catholic churches.

A Catholic herself, Kay's faith in God seemed never to waiver. She was able to transcend the misery of her early life to attain contented sobriety through the practices of service, prayer, forgiveness, patience, compassion and simplicity.

Kay remained active and never drifted away from her AA program in all her 41 years of sobriety. She sponsored dozens of women who called her regularly and stuck with the program. Many of these women have been in her life for decades.

I met Kay in the mid-1980s while my first sponsor, Pat S., was dying of cancer in New York City. Kay was one of many women in orbit around Pat during the final three years of her young life. I was privileged to meet these women and experience, for the first time the kind of caring we see in the program when AA members are sick or in trouble. By the time of Pat's death at age 43, these strong AA women had adopted me. We held each other up and cried together at Pat's funeral. I knew I would choose one of them to be my next sponsor. I never regretted my choice.

Kay met her AA sponsor, Ruth, at her very first AA meeting in the Bronx in 1970. Ruth had one year of sobriety at the time. They maintained their sponsorship relationship until the end. Ruth moved far away from New York City and much of their relationship was conducted across many miles by telephone and periodic meetings or AA conventions. In 1989, I moved away from the city and followed suit.

Kay and I spoke often on the phone. We sometimes visited or met up at conventions.

So it was that I got to know Kay through stories and the stories of those close to her. Through listening to these stories, I came to feel part of my AA lineage and to witness principles of the AA program at work in daily life.

Stories from her 60-year nursing career inspired me to become a nurse myself. She had a special capacity to empathize with her patients and the staff she supervised. She had an ability to meet people where they were, rather than expecting them to step out of their own comfort zone. I am reminded of a story she told me of her work as a nurse.

One day she visited a poor Cambodian family living in the South Bronx. They did not speak English. The only furniture she could see in the apartment was a wooden kitchen chair. The family bid her to sit in this chair and they brought her a glass of water. A young woman had recently given birth to her baby in the apartment. The infant was presented proudly to Kay, in a wool cap with holes cut for the baby's legs, because the family did have any diapers or baby clothes.

The thing I remember most vividly about the telling of this story is the intonation of Kay's voice. She had a way of conveying such intensity of emotion in a contained way and in very few words. As she told me this story, I was brought to tears by the compassion, sorrow, empathy and amazement in her tone.

Kay was a remarkable listener, too. And anything shared with her was held in the strictest confidence.

I don't recall that we ever hugged. She was not physically demonstrative or what we would now call "touchy feely," but she had a way of communicating all she felt through eye contact, facial expression, meaningful silent pauses and tone of voice. Her skillful attention made me feel I was the only other person on the planet, that we had all the time in the world, and that she was in my corner about all things absolutely.

As the "Twelve and Twelve" describes, Kay did not "wallow in emotionalism" nor had she "mistaken it for true religion feeling." She was the genuine article. She was as true a renunciate as any nun, priest or monk I have ever known. Her "order" remains unknown to me. I am certain there were vows taken with her Higher Power. They were evident in the way she practiced our AA principles in her daily life, in the myriad stories she told me, in the skillful attention she showed as we shared our experience, strength and hope with one another.

I owe my life to AA and to this remarkable woman. Her departure from my life was a rite of passage into my AA adulthood. As I write these words I make my own vow ... to try to pass on to others what she, so freely, gave to me.

Chaula H.
Pittsfield, Massachusetts

Not My Choice
November 2007

I didn't pick my sponsor and I didn't particularly like her when I met her. But I was in treatment again, and when I was preparing to leave, the treatment team asked me if I had a sponsor. I said no—but I'd be sure to get one once I got out.

Knowing that that was probably not going to happen, the treatment team assigned me a temporary sponsor. I was set to meet her at an Alcoholics Anonymous meeting the day I was discharged. Amazingly enough, I followed through and met Kathy S. for the first time at a clubhouse in Tallahassee, Florida, on November 3, 1990. As soon as I saw her, I knew we had nothing in common.

She was a fifth-grade schoolteacher. I was a biker babe. She wore colorful clothes with matching accessories. I always wore black and my accessories were chains and a switchblade. She rarely cursed. It was six months before I learned to use the word "mother" by itself. She had her life together and mine was spiraling out of control. I did not listen to what she said, and I did not stay sober.

With her help and guidance, I went back to treatment in January 1991. Since that day, I have not found it necessary or worthwhile to take a drink. I learned a lot in treatment and decided to put the suggestions I had been given into practice.

Although I was stark raving mad, Kathy was willing to work with me. In time, I began to trust her. In all of the years we have worked together, she has never led me astray. I have never been asked me to do anything detrimental or bad for me as a recovering alcoholic and human being.

She taught me about "the box" in life. "The box" was empty and had nothing inside. Kathy said I was settling for it. She told me that I deserved all the pretty tissue paper in different colors, the brilliant wrapping paper, and the luxurious bows—and the gifts that could come inside the box.

She taught me that gifts are not necessarily material goods. Sometimes, gifts couldn't be seen, only felt. For instance: The gift of a good night's sleep, the gifts of integrity, self-respect and the ability to value myself as a human being. My sponsor taught me that I deserved to recover and I was worthy of all the gifts that sobriety had to offer. But these things didn't happen overnight. Just like the Promises in the Big Book, I had to work for them.

I made a lot of meetings, I worked the Steps, I found a Higher Power, I made amends and I tried to help others. Somewhere along the line, I began to find myself. I exchanged my colorful language for colorful clothes. I found the gifts of laughter, friendship and peace of mind. The woman who was once cloaked in black was left behind.

My sponsor saw each triumph. She watched me while I went back to college and earned a degree. She was by my side when I was granted a full pardon from the governor of Florida for the things I had done—the wreckage of my past.

My sponsor also was present during my times of grief and pain. When my son was arrested shortly before Christmas 1997, I was devastated. What kind of gift was that—and right before Christmas? But Kathy showed me the gift I'd received: I found I could handle myself with dignity and grace, something I had known nothing about before. And I didn't have to drink over it.

My sponsor also taught me to accept life on life's terms, that the universe did not revolve around me. (Sometimes, I still argue with that one!) She told me to accept responsibility for my behavior.

It's been a few 24 hours since Kathy and I first met. We have been through a lot together and I know that without her wonderful wisdom and gentle touch, I wouldn't be the woman I am today.

I've since moved to another state and I don't see her much. I've traded Harleys for horses and my switchblade for a hoof pick. But I will never trade my time with Kathy. She is always with me, wherever I go.

Susan K.

Asheville, North Carolina

Grapevine Online Exclusive
Pearl and the Pigeon
July 2014

My sponsor Pearl was quite a tough old bird. One day, she called and said she was taking me to a meeting just outside of town. I climbed into the front seat of her pickup truck and between us sat a very drunk woman. Our pigeon was ranting and rambling and making no sense at all.

Pearl ordered her to be quiet or she'd fasten her to the spare tire on the front of the truck. Pearl explained that as an active drunk, the woman had nothing of value to say and when we got to the meeting, she was to put a cork in it and listen. Surprisingly, this woman did as Pearl told her to do.

On the way home, our drunk was starting to sober up enough so that some of what we were saying about the program was getting through to her cloudy brain. We took her to meetings every night of the week. This necessitated going out of town because back then, Kelowna only had three or four meetings a week, not like the 40 we have now.

We became great friends, attending meetings, roundups and re-treats together. By then, the rewards of sobriety starting happening and her family wanted her back in their lives. Her children wanted her to move to the Island and live with them.

Many years earlier, when I was a rebellious teenager, I lived with a foster family in Ontario. I was a handful—drinking at every oppor-tunity. I was delighted that my foster mom did the same. She taught me that ladies never iron without a glass of wine on the ironing board. She also taught me that as long as we only drank beer and wine, we could never be alcoholics.

My foster father on the other hand enjoyed a few beers while watching the Saturday night hockey game. He had threatened me many times, saying that one night I wasn't going to make it home by my curfew and when I finally arrived, I wouldn't find them there. I thought it was a big joke until one morning I wandered in 12 hours late and discovered an empty apartment. Everything was gone except a garbage bag containing all my belongings.

I went crying to the neighbors and they said that my foster family had left late at night. I guess they had waited for me to come home. He said he gathered that they had a job on the East Coast. I was dev-astated that they would be so fed up with my antics that they would move as far away from me as they could.

In the ensuing years, during periods of sobriety, I would search for them, venturing to the Maritimes and checking phonebooks for their names. They had become part of my Eighth and Ninth Steps and I desperately wanted to find them. In spite of all the times I was read the riot act, I was truly loved and accepted by this family.

Fate intervened. During another period of sobriety, I was invited to attend a wedding on the West Coast. While staying with relatives, I volunteered to peel potatoes for supper. I was given an old newspaper to put the peelings on. As I spread it out, my eye caught the obituar-ies and the name of my foster family. A relative of theirs had died and they were mentioned as survivors, They were living in a small town on Vancouver Island. My heart leapt with joy though I was sure in my heart that they wouldn't want anything to do with me.

This town was the same town where Pearl's pigeon was moving to join her family. I felt certain that if my foster mom were alive, she would have to be in AA. So I gave my friend her name and asked her to keep an eye out for her at meetings. This kept my friend from falling through the cracks. She immediately got hold of AA and immersed herself in meetings, determined to find my foster mom for me while meeting new friends and staying active in the program.

Then, the phone call came. My foster family did want contact! I was so excited and soon after took one of my wee daughters with me and we travelled to the Island by bus to meet her newly acquired grandparents. What a reunion.

And now for the rest of that story. Pop loved the horse races as much as Mom loved her booze, and he'd borrowed some money from the wrong people—more than he could repay. Their leaving that night had nothing to do with me at all. Saying that they were heading east was a ruse; they were heading west the whole time.

There were many visits back and forth over the years and I was able to be there sober for my foster family when Pop got cancer and later passed away. Some time later, Mom remarried—to a boozer—and away went her sobriety. It was a rough time because she didn't want contact with me. Then she had a stroke, which left her paralyzed and living in a care facility. I was able to visit her and see the joy in her eyes when I showed up. I renewed my friendship with my foster brother and his family. They have been a loving support in my life when my birth family rejected me.

All these blessings in my life because my sponsor chose to remember: When anyone reaches out, the hand of AA should be there and for that, she was responsible. Who knows what would have happened had Pearl told that woman that day to call back when she was sober. We say, "Don't quit before the miracle." I am sober and grateful today because I stuck in there and a miracle did happen in my life.

Phyll T.
Parry Sound, Ontario

Every Second Counts
February 1998

I have loved every gal I've ever sponsored and always learned valuable lessons from each of them, none more obvious than the lessons learned from a woman named Rose.

Born Italian and Catholic, Rose was a warm, gregarious person by nature who got sober at 50. She came to me fresh out of rehab and asked me to be her sponsor. It was obvious she'd taken the First Step and we went through the next two quickly. She was so eager to get on with things so we talked about setting out on her Fourth Step. She called me the following day and we met for lunch. "Am I doing this right?" she asked, pulling a sheaf of handwritten paper out of her purse.

She read and I listened. She had made a mighty beginning. "When did you do all this?" I said. "I thought you had a particularly long day at work yesterday."

"I did," she said, "but this was important and I worked on this instead of having dinner."

I was impressed. She had already covered much of her childhood and early years in school. I explained to her that she also needed sleep and food because she needed to be alert on the job—she was an anesthesiologist.

But there was no slowing her down. She called a few more times for lunch meetings and within a short time we were past the Fifth Step and working on the character defects which had shown up in the Fourth. Her quest for as much of the AA program as was humanly possible was nearly daunting to me, but I'm stubborn too, and I felt myself growing through all this.

Rose glowed. She had it—there could be no doubt. When she shared in meetings it was as though we were listening to a real old-timer. She said it was because of all the therapy she had been in over the years. We had fun mapping her Eighth and Ninth Step plans.

Then one day she announced she had a new sponsor, a priest. She needed to move ahead spiritually and she wanted more than I could give. I was crushed at first, but after talking this over with my husband (my sponsor in times of dire crisis), I realized that there was nothing I could do about this but let go of Rose. Outwardly accepting, but inwardly seething at times, I finally realized I couldn't be everyone's sponsor and I had other sponsees who needed me.

At meetings we attended together I noticed a palpable change in Rose. Her inner beauty and peace seemed permanently reflected in her countenance. She began to sponsor people. Her children moved to town just to be close to her and one got in a recovery program of his own. Her job took on a new dimension. In short, she became an AA poster child—all this within the space of 18 months and much of it without my help.

I sulked a bit. My own son was still out there. My finances were a disaster. "Why, God?" I asked. "Why don't I have what Rose has? I've been working five years longer at these things and I've tried to do my best with the Steps." I got no reply.

But I knew that my prayers were tinged with envy, and so I began to pray for Rose as I had prayed for other persons I'd resented.

Then one day the phone rang and it was a friend of mine in the Fellowship who was a nurse in intensive care. "I thought you'd want to know that Rose is here—she's dying. She suffered a massive stroke at work about an hour ago. Her children are here. I can't believe it," she said.

I sat down, stunned, by the phone. I realized that Rose had received what she needed when she needed it. She took a cram course in AA because she didn't have the time to acquire years and years of experience. I delivered a eulogy at her service and said a final goodbye to my friend. I also said goodbye to envy—even of spiritual things.

Mindy S.
LaBelle, Florida

Strawberry Pie Ambush
May 2010

Having been sober less than two years, I have two mother hens who look out after me like I am their baby chick. One is my sponsor; the other is a woman who has been sober longer than I have been on this earth.

Last night they invited me over for strawberry pie. I soon realized this visit had nothing to do with the pie. They each shared their experience regarding alcohol and how cunning, baffling and powerful it is if you are not on guard.

One of them told of how she was 14 months sober and went to the store to buy bread and cereal. She ended up with a six-pack of beer, which she drank before even thinking about what she was doing. She called her husband to tell him what she had done. She asked, "Are you going to leave me over this?" Her husband replied, "It depends on what you do from today forward." She then entered a treatment facility and has been in Alcoholics Anonymous and sober ever since.

They also told me that there are points in sobriety where people can take it for granted and edge the Higher Power out. They go to fewer meetings, and before they know it, they are drinking again.

This was hard for me to fathom, as every time a see a liquor bottle or pass a liquor store I still think about my drinking and my sobriety. I was told it does and can happen. I was given many examples of times when it did happen to people, some of whom never returned to AA.

Their point was how important it is to go to meetings regularly and build up an insurance policy so this can't happen. She went to the store to buy bread and cereal. She ended up with a six-pack of beer, which she drank before even thinking about what she was doing.

It was all directed at me, because my two mother hens could see that life was wearing on me and that I had not been sticking to my meeting schedule. As I left, after we ate our strawberry pie, I was told by hen number one, "I'm proud of you and I expect to hear from you every morning," and by hen number two, "I think you need three meetings a week. Call me when you are leaving a meeting."

I was up bright and early and ended up in two meetings today. I walked into my home group and there was a woman who was returning after having slipped and been out drinking. As the topic went around the room, it ended up being about that insurance policy and how to keep this from happening. That woman had her mother hen sponsor sitting by her, lovingly nudging her along. People spoke of all the bad stuff they had gone through and not found it necessary to drink over because they put their sobriety first. How amazed they were that they could get through what had happened to them without drinking. How grateful they were that they had the entire group to help them along.

When it got around the room to me, I told of my previous night's experience and what I called "the strawberry pie ambush." I told them that, as always, God speaks to me through others, and that he was giving me a double whammy by having this message told to me twice. I also said that having people in my life who care so much about me that they catch me before I have a slip and bring me back to where I need to be makes me feel loved and cared for; like I truly belong.

I left there and promptly called hen one and hen two. Hen two asked what the meeting was about. I told her and she laughed and said, "God speaks to us and we hear what we need to hear!" I asked her what it was like always being right about things and with her southern drawl she said, "Hell, I don't know; I've been right all my life!" Then another big laugh came out.

I went to the evening meeting and saw some folks from the morning. They joked about my being at a second meeting in one day now that I'd had my "talking to." I laughed. One of them said, referring to my "strawberry pie ambush," "Boy, I bet that pie was good."

I said, "Yes, the pie was good, but what I got with it was even better!"

Mary S.
Overland Park, Kansas

CHAPTER FIVE

Beyond Her Wildest Dreams

—————— * ——————

Recovery making powerful changes in the lives of AA women

Some women's lives begin to change the minute they step over the thresholds of AA. Others need more time. The stories in this chapter highlight the subtle and dramatic changes that recovery can bring, sometimes quickly, sometimes slowly.

In the story "A Lady After All," Sharon F. will never forget the ratty mink stole she liked to wear bar-hopping to feel "like a lady," nor the gun she wore on her hip to her first AA meeting. Today, she says she has found "a piece of mind I never dreamed possible."

In "A Minority Of One," an African-American lesbian overcomes doubt about what she has to offer others, whether romantic partners, family members or fellow AAs. She leans heavily on the Ninth Step: "No matter how far down the scale we have gone, we will see how our experience can benefit others."

Member Skeeter S. suffers through multiple suicide attempts before getting sober in AA in her 70s, which she recounts with gratitude and delight in her story, "Never Too Late."

A sober mother of little means moves to a new state with her children to escape her unstable husband in "A Matter of Choice." She leans on her new sponsor, her new sober community and a Higher Power and, one step at a time, makes a new life for her and herself family.

A Lady After All
June 1999

From the age of five, I always felt different than anyone else. I was taller than everybody else, felt uglier than everybody else, and as an only child, I knew I was lonelier than everybody else. I could never measure up to my expectations and I didn't think I measured up to anyone else's either.

My first drink was at age 13. I drank homemade dandelion wine with my alcoholic great-aunt. Suddenly, I was Ginger Rogers, Marilyn Monroe and Eve Arden all rolled into one. I had arrived.

I didn't drink again until my wedding day, five years later. I remember very little about that day. After that, I found that if I drank I could fit in with a crowd; I could be part of a group instead of a loner. I drank to have sex. I drank with my husband and at my husband. I drank in joy, in sadness, in anger. I just drank.

Next came the first divorce, and I was the original party girl from then on. I found myself crawling in and out of different barroom bathroom windows, running away from my actions. I'd sit on a barstool in my ratty mink stole, the hem of my skirt tucked into my girdle, thinking I was "hip, slick, and cool." I was a lady, after all. I drank wearing a mink stole, so I had to be a lady. I ended up in strange places with strange men and thought I was having the time of my life. Often, I had to call someone the next day to see if I had indeed had a good time!

In 1960, I went on the wagon for several years. I was living in the Canadian bush, 50 miles from the nearest town and neighbor. It was too far to go for a drink, especially in the winter and 20 feet of snow. Finally I moved to a small town in British Columbia and met a lady who offered to teach me to knit at the pub every afternoon. Of course, I had to be sociable and hoist a pint or two. I controlled my drinking until I could get home to "Harvey"—Harvey's Bristol Cream Sherry, that is. I thought I was in hog heaven since I was drinking like a lady: everybody knows that ladies drink sherry.

I returned to the United States in 1968, and my drinking career continued. I'd go to work with a big brown aspirin bottle full of Canadian Club whiskey in my purse for emergencies. After work, I'd stop for a quick one and invariably my son would have to call, hours later, begging me to come home. This continued through another marriage.

In 1974, we moved to Southern California, and I immediately hated the Mojave Desert and all of California. I realized I'd lose my paycheck (my hubby) if I didn't slow down on the booze. I discovered prescription drugs could help me, although alcohol was my drug of choice. Hubby would take care of me if I was "sick" but not if I was a drunk. I ended up with a fifth-a-day habit, and a $600-a-month pharmacy bill. I was going to three doctors and two hospitals. The blackouts were beginning again but I was just "sick." I didn't have a drinking problem—not me. I was having trouble on the job, in my marriage, with my family, with other men, with finances—everything except with the law. That was because I was married to a law-enforcement officer. I once ended up in an airline terminal in Minneapolis, Minnesota, dressed in the same ratty mink stole, talking about going ice fishing. I came home and tried to straighten up.

I went back to church, read every self-help book I could find, but that didn't last long. Soon I was back in the bars, trying to work, keep Hubby from knowing what I was doing, and still party heavily.

My next major blackout found me in Jeddi, Saudi Arabia. I'm told that I dared some airline pilots to smuggle me into Saudi Arabia to see just how red the Red Sea was. It isn't red, but a beautiful blue, away from shore. It took a week to smuggle me out of the country and back to Los Angeles.

Then I knew I needed help, but I had to go to one more party. Again, I experienced another blackout. I was told on my 19th AA anniversary that I had been evicted from the San Bernardino chapter of the Hell's Angels for being too crazy. The man who evicted me was celebrating 13 years of continuous sobriety that evening.

I was getting sicker—physically and emotionally. Spiritually, I was dead. I had reached the point where I couldn't live but I couldn't die. My only son, the apple of my eye, finally confronted me with an ultimatum. "Mother, either you get help now, or I will leave and you will never hear or see me again as long as you live," he told me. Somehow I knew he meant it. I called the crisis hotline and was in the hospital a few hours later. My fear of losing my son was great enough that I would ask for help from anyone. It took 30 days to detox from the alcohol and drugs before I walked into my first meeting of Alcoholics Anonymous.

I entered that meeting weighing 320 pounds, standing six feet tall, wearing tight blue jeans, a western shirt, cowboy boots, a Stetson hat, and a .45 pistol on my hip. Slapping the gun on the table, I said, "All right, you turkeys, I want what you have, this thing you call sobriety." A small man with a big bushy mustache slid the gun away from me and growled, "Sit down and shut up. I'll tell you when, where and if you can talk." I promptly did what he said, and it was the first direction I had taken in a long time.

The group told me: "Keep coming back. Don't drink between meetings. Bring the body, the mind will follow. Put the plug in the jug. Take the cotton out of one ear, put that cotton in your mouth. Leave the cotton in one ear only so what you hear won't whistle through that empty cavity. Be willing to put as much energy into your sobriety as you put into your drinking. You have a disease called alcoholism. If you were a diabetic, you probably would be taking insulin. The medicine for alcoholism is AA and you need to take a dose daily." I was told to take it one day at a time—"But if a day is too long, cut it down." I was told to attend 30 meetings in 30 days. At the end of 30 days, I was told, "Since you are such a sick puppy, you need to re-up' for another 30 days." They kept harping on "Keep Coming Back." It had been years since I had been asked to return anywhere. My thought was, I'll fix them, I will go back.

Members told me I needed to be willing to go to any length for my sobriety. That meant if necessary, giving up husbands, children, jobs, houses, cars, friends, etc., to stay sober. I was to get a sponsor, a person who walked her talk, one I respected. I didn't have to like her; liking would come later.

I was now in school, a school to learn how to live life without booze. The Big Book of Alcoholics Anonymous was my textbook, and I was to read the first 164 pages only. I was not to memorize it. "Always have to search for what you want to find, that way you will learn more each time you pick up the book, no matter how long you are in the Fellowship," I was told. "This way you will learn to live the Twelve Steps and Twelve Traditions and not become an AA guru."

I also was told to be at a meeting 15 minutes early and stay 15 minutes late. I was to ask questions, listen and socialize with those who had more continuous sobriety. I was to strive for quality sobriety, for often quality would bring quantity. I was to work the Twelve Steps and Twelve Traditions to the best of my ability. "Honesty comes with practice", they said, "and this thing called sobriety comes with practice, too."

People suggested that I needed a Higher Power or my sobriety might not last. I'd been a church member for years, but I didn't have a personal relationship with my Higher Power, whom I choose to call God, until then.

I was also told, "Your first year is a gift." In my first year, my stepfather died, and I was bitten by a rattlesnake and a black widow spider. I had a heart attack and a stroke. My three stepchildren were killed by a drunk driver. I went to meetings, did not drink and used the Fellowship of AA to get me through that first year. If the first year was a gift—thank you, but no more gifts. I will work for my sobriety and will continue to do so as long as I live.

Today, I can face death (mine as well as that of others), remarriages and illness. I'm able to accept responsibility for others and myself. I can face poverty as well as affluence. I'm employable, adaptable and teachable—thanks to the program of Alcoholics Anonymous and God. I'm learning to live life on life's terms and to enjoy it. To accept the good and the bad, and to be grateful for both. I have a long way to go, and

I pray I never give up growing spiritually, emotionally and mentally.

This program will work for you too, if you keep coming back. Don't drink or use between meetings. Be willing to be willing to follow directions and you will find your life changing in all areas. Today, I don't have the home, the husband, the three cars in the garage. I have one old clunker that takes me to meetings. I am not financially well-off, but I have a peace of mind I never dreamed possible. My needs are always met—and even some of my wishes. I am truly happy for the first time in my life. Thank you, AA. Today I am a real lady.

Sharon F.
Milwaukie, Oregon

Gay, Joyous and Free
October 2012

Coming to terms with my own sexual identity as a lesbian was at the heart of my alcoholism. I knew from a very early age that I liked girls in the same way that boys liked girls. Growing up in the 60s and becoming a teen in the 70s was not yet a safe time period to reveal my true sexual orientation. Alcohol offered me an illusory relief—a way to drown the secret, sinful feelings and keep them down under. This became a vicious cycle: each crush on a woman was doused in booze; each bout of drinking jumbled my thinking and found me confusing benign friendly gestures by female friends as something more, perhaps even romantic. I would "act out" sexually and quite promiscuously with men I met in bars, all the while fantasizing about women—and the drinking progressed.

My first relationship with a woman occurred just six weeks before I got sober. Interestingly enough, I met her when she was in the beginning of a relapse after having been sober for seven years. It was a disaster in the making, yet there was a divine orchestration underneath: put two alcoholics together and watch their drinking double! My Higher Power put her in my path, I believe, to bring me swiftly to my bottom. Within a few months, she too would seek sobriety.

I was 28 years old when I came out as a lesbian and took my last drink. The year was 1990. Putting the bottle down, however, did not automatically mend all the pieces of the broken person I was when I arrived at AA. My self-esteem dragged behind me on the floor like a worn-out mop. I still carried shame about being a lesbian, having been rejected by several so-called friends (and former drinking buddies). The clubhouse I went to was a male-dominated meeting, so I did not feel comfortable identifying myself as a lesbian, nor did I really want to be there because I did not want to identify as an alcoholic either! I came to meetings late, left early, never got a sponsor or picked up a single piece of literature. My ego and my self-will told me that I was the one who was in charge of putting down my last drink, therefore I was also the one who could "graduate" myself from meetings two years later!

I stayed away from meetings for 16½ years. I lived a dry, anxiety-ridden, ego-driven life, playing God. A major financial bottom brought me back to the rooms of AA in 2009—only this time with my head held high. For the first time ever, I identified myself as an alcoholic. Within a few short weeks of daily meetings, I acknowledged that I was a lesbian. No one batted an eye. In fact, I "came out" at a predominantly male, African-American meeting (I am Caucasian), sharing my story of experience, strength and hope. In the midst of my story, I did this dramatic pause and whispered the words, "I knew I was gay," bracing for the looks of judgment and ridicule. Instead, the entire front row, in an exaggerated manner, held their hands to their faces and shouted "No! Not that!" The room burst out into fits of laughter. It was not only safe for me to come out, but it was embraced!

For the past three-plus years, I have been fully committed to my recovery and membership in AA. And it is with great humility that I share the story of my inner turmoil regarding my sexual identity and its connection to my alcoholism. In doing this, I hope to help other alcoholics who have experienced or are experiencing this same struggle to know that they are not alone and that AA is one place that is guaranteed not to turn them away.

My life has never been better. I am truly gay, joyous and free in AA.

K.A.

Philadelphia, Pennsylvania

Nice Jewish Girls Don't Go to Prison
July 2002

I grew up in a typical American household—Mom was the homemaker and Dad went out to work. We celebrated all the Jewish holidays, and I don't remember that alcohol was ever a problem at any of the family functions. However, I do remember my father drinking a lot and keeping his alcohol on a shelf above the telephone in the kitchen—and that was off limits for us.

I had my first drunk at my brother's wedding when I was 14. The wedding was at a fancy Jewish country club in Houston, Texas. I threw up on my dress. My mom was not happy with me, and I was sent home.

When I turned 15, I met my first love. My parents used to let us drink at their house, and we thought that was cool. In Houston in those days, if you were a good little Jewish girl, you went to Israel when you were 17. I was there when I found out that my father had left my mother. (He'd actually left her the day he had dropped me off at the airport.) My cousin, who was on the trip with me, held me as I cried. That night he took me out, and we drank vodka and orange juice.

When I came home to Texas, my life had completely changed. In addition to my parents divorcing, my boyfriend was entering a premed program and his parents had convinced him that he'd be better off if we didn't see one another. Three months later, my cousin shot himself in the head. It took me a long time to get over his death.

College came next, but when I didn't get good grades, my father sent me to work, where my boss, a cocaine addict, introduced me to snorting cocaine. I stopped using after going to my ear, nose and throat doctor for a check-up though, because he told me that if I didn't, I would ruin his creation—my nose job. Then I went to work for a health center in Houston and started taking diet pills. I also started writing my own prescriptions. Fortunately, I didn't get caught—that time.

When I was 26, I met the man of my dreams: the UPS man. As it turned out, he delivered more than packages. A former IV user, he was now an active drinker, and when he introduced me to martinis, I thought I had died and gone to paradise. I was hooked immediately. From that moment on, we were bound together by vodka and foggy love. The first Fourth of July we spent together, he was arrested for public intoxication, and I was sent home. Of course, I bailed him out of jail and told him that I never wanted to see him again. We moved in together shortly after that. His two-year-old daughter moved in with us as well, and I took on the role of mommy.

On the day of our wedding, in the synagogue I had grown up in, I was severely hungover, and our entire honeymoon, a trip to the Napa Valley, was a total drinkfest. The video of the trip could be used to show the progression of alcoholism.

The following years were hard. I crossed that invisible line with my drinking right before I got pregnant, and I found not drinking when I was pregnant rough. So, I drank. I knew it was wrong, but I couldn't stop. I had no idea that I was an alcoholic. Why would I? I drank a gallon of milk each day to provide nutrition to counteract the alcohol. (Later, when I read the story in the Big Book about the man who drank whiskey and washed it down with milk, I could relate.) I was doing so much research on the internet about fetal alcohol syndrome that I was practically an expert. But I still drank when I came home from work. The insidiousness of the disease had a hold on me. I even drank the morning I delivered my son. Lennie was born four weeks prematurely, with hyaline membrane disease (prematurity of the lungs), and we spent the next four weeks in the neonatal unit. My husband said at the time, "If anything is wrong with him, I will never forgive you." I was filled with so much guilt that I could hardly stand it. I had to drink. I had to numb the overwhelming hole in my heart.

Crushed when I had to go home from the hospital without my baby, I sat beside his empty cradle every night and cried. I had not bonded with my son, and I was so afraid of the damage I thought I had done to him. The chief neonatologist told me that Lennie was fine; the damage that had been done was because of his prematurity. But I still had a hard time accepting that. The therapist I was seeing at the time begged me to tell the doctor about my drinking, but I just couldn't bring myself to do it—I was too scared.

The day I could finally take my baby home, I cried so hard with joy that I could hardly see. I swore off liquor and thanked God. But that did not keep me sober.

The scary day came when I was taking a shower, and the baby ran out the front door and around the block by himself. I found him in the arms of the lady at the gas station. I was devastated and ashamed. I was also hungover. When I got home, I phoned my sister-in-law and told her what had happened. Two hours later, she and my brother were at my door, ready to take me to the hospital to get help for my drinking.

Once we got there, my sister-in-law told the medical staff what had happened, and within five minutes, Child Protective Services arrived. I begged my brother to take me home, and I left, vowing never to drink again. The next day, my husband told me that if I didn't check into another hospital, he would divorce me. So I went, but I checked myself out within the four hours allowed for voluntary leave.

My mother, who was suffering from the neurological disorder Huntington's chorea, was living across the bayou from us now. She too was drinking and roaming the streets at night. After she was admitted to the psych ward (the same one I had been in), I told my brother I needed some help with her: I was losing it, trying to hold myself together, take care of my mother, a new baby and a little girl, and drink.

I was also still holding onto my job. Then, on "Take Your Daughter to Work Day," I took my daughter to work—drunk. The next day, I checked into Spring Shadows Glen for 28 days of treatment. I was told that I was an alcoholic. Not me I said, until I drank my hair spray. That's when I realized there was something very wrong with me.

After 28 days, I went home, went on vacation and drank again. I could not get sober and was baffled. I started to drink hair spray quite frequently and became violently sick. My husband took me to a women's center, but I ran away the next day. I was absolutely out of my mind. I was run down and beat up from alcohol, but that did not stop me. I drank again.

Then my AA angel made a Twelfth Step call on me, and she and another AA took me to a women's center in Pasadena. This place was the real deal. Filled with straight-off-the-street women, it took my soul straight away. That's the only way I can describe it. I kept telling my husband, "I'm going to die here." That's how I truly felt. But everyone kept telling him to leave me out there.

When I finally did return home, I was numb. My husband and I attended an AA meeting that night, and I got a sponsor. The next day in my backyard, I felt the spirit move through me and I fell to my knees, begging for help. I was so sick and so tired of truly being sick and tired.

I started to sober up. But when the weight I had lost after delivering the baby started coming back on, I began taking diet pills. I was soon addicted to them. I was eating diet pills during AA meetings and coming home and smoking pot. Needless to say, I started drinking again. I also started to write fake prescriptions. Then one day it happened: I was arrested. Fortunately, I did not have my son with me. I was taken to jail, and my husband arrived around midnight with my little girl to get me out. I was severely depressed and frightened. I thought I was going to prison. Nice Jewish girls don't go to prison.

I was facing a deferred adjudication felony sentence and was scared out of my mind. I started to drink again and went to pretrial drunk. Luckily, the judge was not there, and I was sent home. I tried to detox myself, but was having a rough time of it. I was shaking violently and throwing up incessantly. That's when my AA angel arrived. She told my husband to buy me a pint of whiskey and get me to the hospital to detox.

When we arrived, I finally understood what was happening to me. I told God, "It's up to you now." But five days later, when my son had an asthma attack and needed medical attention, I left. It was before my court date, but I thought it would be OK because I was under a doctor's care. Wrong. My attorney told me that the judge would call back the warrant if I checked into treatment for another 28 days. We had no more insurance left and I began to panic. I begged my husband to let me put my treatment on his credit card. This was not going over well with him at all, but I checked into a center that Thursday. Unfortunately, the paperwork and the warrant got crossed, and I was arrested the next day. My attorney promised he would have me out that night. I ended up spending a week in the county jail, but I was sober, and I told myself that this was the end of my old life. Some women there kept me safe. I prayed and attended two AA meetings, and I knew what I had to do: stay sober.

When I was released, my brother took me back to treatment. The next day, my husband served me divorce papers. I was crushed. He said I was financially breaking the family, but I knew that he had just had enough of the lies and the chaos. I went back to work and was graciously "let go." My job had ended, I was moving again, and I was getting divorced. But I was sober.

Satisfied with my treatment, the court sentenced me for a deferred adjudication felony with two years' probation and Prison for a Day. I was taken to a women's prison in Dayton, Texas, for the scared-straight program. It did scare me—straight out of my mind, but I didn't drink. God had removed the obsession from me, and I was following suggestions given to me by my sponsor and everyone around me.

My home group became my safe haven, and I was able to go back to work—as a school secretary at the synagogue where I was consecrated as a kindergartner, bat mitzvahed as a young teen, and married. I guess God wanted me where he could keep an eye on me.

Here and in the rooms of AA I have started to put my life together, and it has changed so much that sometimes I shake my head and say, "What was that all about?" Now that we are divorced, my ex-husband and I are great friends as we go about life raising our children. I have also moved into a new apartment. It is small but just right for me.

I am still reminded of the consequences of my alcoholism once a month when I go to my probation officer. The good news is that it's almost stress-free because I am sober. I go to at least four or five meetings a week and I have never been more content.

My meetings and my Step work are my first priorities—even over my son. I take a meeting to a women's center twice a month. It brings me back to where I used to be. And I have a sponsor who has been there for me my entire sobriety and pre-sobriety. Determined to help me get sober, she made numerous Twelfth Step calls on me. Without her help and guidance, I wouldn't be here today. I also met a gentleman with 17 years of dedicated and very grateful sobriety who taught me how to use the Steps in everyday life and how to live again. He has taught me to stay in the reality of life, to look at things for what they really are and not what I want them to be.

Most importantly, I use the Third Step every day of my life. If I can turn my will and my life over to the care of God, then that takes a lot of pressure off me. You see, it's not up to me at all any more. My sobriety is a gift from God.

My biggest fear is that my son will be with a bunch of his friends and their mothers and say, "My mommy is just glad to be sober today." Then I have a vision of that, and it cracks me up. After all, he is right.

Sherri B.
Houston, Texas

A Matter of Choice
September 2005

I am so grateful for sponsorship in the program of Alcoholics Anonymous. Without it, I would never have made it.

Women sponsors have taught me how to live life on life's terms. There have been many times during my 13-year sober journey when I have gone on the faith that my sponsor had. When I don't see the way through the fog, and when it just seems too hard, God works through others to let me know that it's OK to move to the next step.

I am a single parent of three children, ages 8, 10 and 12. I moved back to California after living in Colorado for two years. The move to Colorado was a last-ditch effort to make a disastrous relationship work; you know, I always have one more great idea ...

I had met this man in the throes of alcoholism and drug addiction. We were really just a couple of kids suffering from this disease, and we didn't even know it. He attempted to throw me out of a moving car on our first date, but that wasn't enough evidence for me to never go out with him again.

While drinking, the abuse was much worse: he fractured my ribs while I was pregnant, held me hostage in a motel room and one time he choked me until I passed out. When I got sober, he decided to quit using and drinking as well, only he did it on his own, without any program. This, as we know in AA, is called dry drunkenness, and it was worse for the family than if he had simply drunk.

But I continued, by the grace of God, to seek help and to try to clear up the wreckage of my past. I was afraid to leave. He had threatened me long ago, saying that if I tried he would hunt me down like a dog and kill me. I believed him. Probably a lot of fear about raising my children alone helped me to stay, even though I was already doing everything on my own.

After one final physical attack, I took my children and left while their father was still in jail. We came to California, driving a moving van full of pots, pans and whatever else I could throw in it. I was a wreck. The kids were wrecks. I hadn't slept with both eyes closed in about a year, and I had constant bladder infections, ulcers—every stress-related disorder you could imagine.

I cried out to God for help, and he started to put teachers into my life. I met my first sponsor in a women's meeting in Fullerton. She helped me to find new ways to support my family using the Seventh Tradition—which states that the AA groups themselves ought to be fully supported by the voluntary contributions of their own members—as a way to live my own life. She promised me that I would begin to feel better as soon as I worked at being less dependent on others both financially and emotionally.

So I started taking classes, first to become a nurse's aide and then a medical assistant. The kids and I slept on the floor of my mother's studio apartment in Brea, so I was fortunate not to have to pay rent. Unfortunately, this was not my attitude at that time! I have had to live with the fact that I complained and whined constantly in meetings about my misfortune. "Poor me," they would all say and then crack up into hysterics. This was all done to help me to get over my huge defect of self-pity, and it worked.

I worked at a gas station as a cashier to have money for food and other necessities. I spent a lot of time studying the Big Book behind that glass window. I learned so much from that job, how to suit up and show up, literally. One of the other problems I had was that I didn't like rules. The gas station uniform needed a little sprucing up, or so I thought. On every shift I would come in with it tied in the front or unbuttoned too low, anything to be different. This caused many unnecessary conflicts with my manager. People in the program said, "Just tuck the shirt in and be nice." So I did, and it worked!

The problem of not sleeping continued long after my arrival in California. Even the kids couldn't sleep. I would wake up in the middle of the night with the sensation of the barrel of a shotgun on my forehead, cold and smooth. Terror ran through my body. I would just shake and sob. I hit my knees in a desperate rendition of the Lord's Prayer, and even if it was in the middle of the night, I called my sponsor. She never yelled at me or treated me like a second-class citizen. In her quiet, relaxed voice she would ask, "What's up?" and I would open up my soul. By the end of the conversation she usually had me laughing so hard about some story from her life that I had forgotten what was wrong with me in the first place. When it was time to hang up, I would say, "Do you think I'll sleep tonight?" and she would say, "I will pray for you. Everything's going to be OK." That stuff is priceless. I believed her, and some time after that, the insomnia started to get better.

I learned the difference between a want and a need from sponsors in the program. My list of things I needed to buy with my paycheck had been something like this: $20 for the tanning booth, $15 for Starbucks, $10 to put gas in the car, $30 for the movies, $20 to take the kids to McDonald's—you know, all the essentials. So it was through much pain and humiliation that I learned to contribute to the rent by giving my mom some money each month, and I quit tanning after one Step study meeting when the subject was on the seven deadly sins. An old-timer said to me afterward, "Talk about vanity—look at that tan you have." I was so hurt, but it worked! Today, it's amazing how little I need to be happy. I think it's the gratitude for what I have that God has put in my heart that's changed me.

I shared constantly about what "he" had done to me, and all the things that "he" continued to do, like not paying child support and yelling at me on the phone. More lessons were to be learned. My sponsor suggested that I go to the district attorney to get child support, which was something that I had a lot of fear about. I'll never forget the feeling of opening the mailbox and seeing a check in it. As also suggested, I put a sign on the wall by the phone that I would be forced to see that said, "Hang up the phone!" When he started to scream or manipulate, I learned to just hang up. It worked!

I can remember one meeting in particular when I was full of self-pity and going on and on about "him" and an old-timer asked, "Well, who picked him, honey?" Well, that really fired me up. I thought to myself, I'll never share about him again! And so I learned to share about what "I" was doing, or, more importantly, not doing.

Then came the time when, after working as a medical assistant and learning how to use money a little more wisely, I got my own place. I really grew up; being the mother and the father, you learn really quickly what's important. I went to work and meetings, I met with my sponsor and did the laundry. I found true happiness and contentment in doing what God wanted me to do.

I had applied for HUD housing years earlier, and finally I got on the program, only the apartment building that we lived in didn't accept HUD funding. So I started to look for one that would and found that many landlords won't take it. My sponsor continued to have faith, even when I had none; she felt sure that I would find a place before the deadline was up. I can still hear her saying, "Sometimes, God waits until the very last hour, even minute, but he will answer." So I went on her faith, just like every other time when I thought things couldn't possibly work out.

The day before HUD was about to expire, I found our condo in Brea. To me, it's paradise. My sponsor used to tell me when I complained about living with my mom, "Fix up the place as much as you can, make it beautiful, and as soon as you really start to like it, it will be time to leave." So I learned how to make a comfortable, safe and loving home for my family and me.

I have gone back to college in an attempt to support my family in a more appropriate way. I never thought this would be possible, but my sponsor kept on encouraging me. Once again, I went on her faith. It has been a struggle with financial insecurity. I don't see how we are getting by, but something always comes through. This semester, I was nominated for a journalism scholarship. Right away, I thought, No way will I get it. They don't know who I am. However, my professor called me this week to let me know that I got the scholarship and that the announcement dinner is this month. This is truly a victory that I owe to the program and, of course, to my God.

My Higher Power gives me wonderful gifts, and he likes to involve a lot of people in the process. Having faith is following through with my sponsor's suggestions even when it doesn't make sense.

I am learning to trust in God and in the program of Alcoholics Anonymous more and more every day, one day at a time.

Kara P.
Brea, California

Never Too Late
March 2002

As I prepare to celebrate my 75th birthday, I am so thankful I've found the happy, joyous and free path in AA. I've spent most of my life running away from problems and always blaming others for my unhappiness. At first, the alcohol made me feel like the life of the party. Then it became a necessity. I was having aches and pains, so the doctors prescribed sleeping pills and pain pills. With all these mind-altering substances, I could escape from reality (or so I thought).

I'd had three separate professional careers, so when I finally retired, I thought my life was over, and I settled down to die at 72. Fortunately (after two suicide attempts), my family, who I thought had deserted me, did an intervention and put me in a rehab center to detox and learn the AA way of life. After 28 days, I thought I was cured. I was gung ho about the program and wanted to tell all comers just how to do it. I got a sponsor, breezed through the Steps and settled down with what I thought was my new career. But when I had a little trouble falling asleep, out would come the pills, and booze soon followed. I was back on the rollercoaster again.

After hearing my daughter tell my grandchildren that this was what a dope fiend looked like, I tried suicide again, but to no avail. Maybe my Higher Power wanted to keep me here a little longer. So I went back to the hospital and the Big Book again, this time for real.

I decided that half measures availed me nothing and maybe I should listen to my sponsor and work the program the right way. I started again on Step One with all my heart, body and soul. This time I went to work with the zeal of a dying woman. Shortly, I was completely changed—I found what people were talking about when they said they were rocketed into the fourth dimension. Never have I known such peace of mind or happiness. I'm now working on my Steps every day. I call my sponsor every day, I have sponsees I am trying to help, I am attending meetings and going to H & I (hospitals and institutions committee) meetings to help those who are trying to get a new way of life.

I'm also volunteering at our central office two mornings a week and am on call to do Twelfth Step work for those women who have reached the end of their rope. I say, "Just tie a knot and hang on. Remember Jonah—he was down in the mouth of the whale, but he came out OK, with the help of God." Every day I wake up, I thank God for a good night's sleep and ask him, "What can I do for you today?"

Remember: It is never too late to get a good life. I am looking forward to many more years of happiness and service.

Skeeter S.
San Antonio, Texas

A Minority of One
October 1997

B y the time I crawled through the doors of Alcoholics Anonymous, I felt like a minority of one. In fact, I had pretty much always felt that way. I was the first child of a loving family with an extended kin network, so where did all of that fear, doubt and insecurity come from? How did the pretty little girl who made all As and sang in the church choir end up as the only woman drunk on a street corner with the guys? Whatever caused it, it was not that I am an African-American or that I am a lesbian.

When I started to drink at age 15 or 16, I drank like an alcoholic. This made me a minority right away, since my peers in high school were not particularly interested in booze. It was the 60s, and shortly after I became a teenaged drunk, I gravitated toward as many of the movements of that era as I could, becoming a black militant hippie peacenik gay activist drunk. All the while I was glorying in my uniqueness. I disputed even those who seemed to understand me because I really needed to be one of a kind: I thought it was all I had.

In 1977, at the age of 27, I finally made it to Alcoholics Anonymous. I'd been to quite a few meetings before that in treatment centers, detoxes and court-ordered circumstances. But it wasn't until 1977, when I ended up with a bottle on a street corner, that it hit me like a hammer that I was at the end of the line. I said a prayer—just a little one, but quite distinct, that came up from someplace deep inside me. It transformed a curse into a cry for help. When I came to, I was in a detox. After that, I spent almost a year in a halfway house, getting sober. Around Easter 1978, I finally surrendered all the way, letting go of the marijuana and the prescribed "mood elevators," and I began to look for a Higher Power.

One of my sponsors used to tell me, when I was feeling especially put upon by members of my own species, "You've got to have people— that's all there is!" Vulnerable, hurt and needy, I sincerely doubted this. But God started to show its face in a parade of people brought before me, usually just at the right time. My first sponsor in AA was the only other black woman AA in the area. We were kind of pushed together even though we didn't have much else in common. We did share alcoholism and the desire to stay sober, and that was enough. This woman told me to call her every day at 6 P.M. sharp, gave me a Big Book and said, "Let's get started" and "Let's grow together."

The first person I sponsored in AA was a gay white man from the South; he was also several years younger than I was. His Higher Power whispered in his ear that I should chair a workshop at the annual gay and lesbian AA round-up on the experience of being a gay person who got sober at "straight" meetings, so he signed both of us up as co-chairs. That workshop was standing-room only.

My first partner in sobriety tried to show me how precious I was, just exactly the way I was at that moment. I wasn't ready for it at the time, but I remember the effort and the love with gratitude. Then, fearful and ashamed, when I was sober a little over three years, I went home to face my family, and they welcomed me with shining eyes, love and forgiveness and lots of hugs.

Somewhere along the line, I'm not sure when, I came to believe that my experiences and who I am have been given to me for the express purpose of passing along a certain message, inside AA and outside of it. As it says in what many call the Promises—what I refer to as "the guarantees," since the book says that they will always materialize if we work for them—"No matter how far down the scale we have gone, we will see how our experience can benefit others." As one of my AA friends likes to say, "God is good."

Some days, I still feel like a minority of one. I go to meetings where it seems that everyone else is sober a few days or a few years, and where to some my double-digit sobriety makes me look like I have all the answers and don't have difficulties or need to make amends. Alcoholism still occasionally whispers from a small place inside me, planting fear, doubt and insecurity if I do not exercise constant vigilance.

I recently moved back to what I sometimes call "the scene of the crime"—the city where I was born and grew up. I feel very sure that I was brought back here for a specific purpose, though I may not be given to know what it is. Perhaps it is to live my amends to my family and old friends, clean up my side of the street going back as far as the story goes. Walking through the doors of an AA meeting today, I feel at home, and love the sound of our many different voices coming together at the end of a meeting to pray the Lord's Prayer or the Serenity Prayer. I am grateful today that God's voice is stronger and surer than my occasional negative whispers, comforting me through difficult times, letting me know that I am part of the whole.

D.E.S.

St. Louis, Missouri

Out of the Nest
March 2014

I found my way up the wooden, rickety stairs of a San Fernando clubhouse in June of 1986. There were five women and eight screaming children, and I was absolutely sure that my life was over. I would never see daylight again that was not filtered through layers of cigarette smoke and the smell of (what I now know is) AA coffee. There would never be fun or laughter again. I would never know another lover or friend who had an ounce of personality, and I would grow old just like those five 40-year-old women I saw sitting around those AA tables.

If any one of those women had tried to tell me about the ride I was embarking upon, I would have called them all liars and stomped down the stairs much quicker than I had climbed up on that hot day in southern California. Those sober women, however, did not try to tell me who I was or what it was going to be like, nor did they shock, belittle or shame me. Had those things happened, I might never have come back. The chairwoman, Peggy, asked my name and asked if I wanted to share. The others said, "Keep coming back," and one of them may have told me that I never had to take another drink, even if I wanted to.

That morning I had called all the people who would normally be available to get loaded before work, but no one showed up at my house. I had run out of alcohol and woken up feeling hopeless and sick again. So I made my first and last deal with a God I did not understand. I needed to go to the market and the laundromat. I had to wash my truck and the house needed to be cleaned. If I could get those done and I had time, I would give up and drive down to that AA meeting I had heard about. I didn't know what I would find there. I only knew that a drunk was someone who drank whiskey and smelled bad. But

I didn't drink whiskey and I showered every day, so I was out of the woods there.

I went to the market and did my laundry, taking as much time as I possibly could. I looked at the clock and it had barely moved. I cleaned my house and washed my truck. The clock had barely moved. I cleaned the oven and even did the bathroom that was my room- mate's responsibility, and the clock didn't move. It seemed pretty clear that that noon meeting had my name all over it, and like it or not I was about to experience AA for the first time.

What had started with a warm six-pack of stolen beer when I was 13, ended with two bottles of beer at a family bowling alley at 23. Dur- ing those 10 years I finished high school, got a good job, dropped out of college, fell in love and started to grow up. Or so I thought. The last two years of my drinking left no doubt that I had crossed a line and was incapable of coming back on my own. The few remaining people who genuinely cared about me were afraid for my future and my health, and were petrified every time I got behind the wheel of my car. I had stopped going to see my family so they could not see what I had become. And anyone who didn't drink like I did no longer had a place in my life. How this middle class girl from the suburbs got to that point was beyond me.

But now I was facing the bottom of the stairs at the clubhouse. I saw really nice handmade woodcarvings of Steps One through Twelve. The Traditions hung on the wall by the kitchen. I didn't know it then, but those two things would come to mean more to me than almost anything else. One of those five women gave me a directory and pointed out that there were meetings at the clubhouse three or more times a day. I had nowhere else to go before or after work and they had air conditioning and toilet paper, so I came back—over and over again for six months.

On Christmas Eve 1986, I took a six-month chip. It reminded me of the poker chips I used to play cards with my dad and his cronies. That little plastic chip meant as much to me as my biweekly pay- checks. I finally got a sponsor, but didn't call her. I started to have a friend or two, but didn't trust them. I continued to go to work, go to meetings, and not do anything that would put me in jeopardy. But I was just OK.

I had a "part-time" relationship that finally ended. Now I was really on my own for the first time as a sober woman, and I had no idea what to do with myself. I practically lived at the clubhouse when I was not at work or sleeping. Around New Year's, that woman who was at my first meeting, Peggy, pulled me aside and suggested that I venture outside the clubhouse. She told me to find meetings with people who looked like me, talked like me and walked like me. It was now time to start building a life in sobriety and not just staying physically sober. It was as if the mother bird was pushing the fledgling out of the nest. It was really difficult. I started to peek at the directory and tried to figure out what was next for me. At 24 years old, I sure didn't feel very grown up.

It was at about this time that the poem "Footprints" came into my life. I was starting to have emotions. I would wake up with feelings and I didn't like it. I was reading the Big Book, calling my sponsor and working the Steps. But I was going from numb to raw. I could not trust myself. I needed someone or something to carry me through. "Footprints" along with the Serenity Prayer and the Third and Seventh Step prayers became my affirmations, my mantras—my bread and butter.

I branched out first to one new meeting, then another. Slowly I found a young people's meeting, then a women's meeting and then a Big Book study. I was invited to coffee, and I went. Helen, my first sponsor, told me to look around me. While I listened I began to watch people cry, laugh, stay sober and sometimes come back after a relapse. I remember being so scared when I heard that men and women in my meetings were drinking again. I wondered why the Higher Power in "Footprints" had not carried them the way I felt I was being carried. My sponsor reminded me that alcoholism is "cunning, baffling, and powerful" and that not everyone makes it.

When my ego got big at nine months, my sponsor sent me to the ocean to try and stop the tide from coming in. I remember hitting my knees on the cold sand that day and crying tears down my cheeks onto my chest. I let out huge sobs that started in the deepest part of my soul and took my breath away before escaping my mouth. It seemed that every emotion I had missed while drinking poured from me on the beach that day. I believe that my obsession to drink was lifted then. I'm one of the lucky ones.

I feel like my story is an expanded version of "Footprints." I have certainly felt my Higher Power carrying me since 1986. But when I was not able to pray as described in the Sixth Step, when I refused to let the light in, there was more than one set of footprints behind me. There were more than two sets. There have been so many people who have carried me over the years.

During the late 80s and early 90s, when so many of my friends were dying from AIDS, members of AA carried me. When our son was born in 1990, and while I learned to become a real parent, partner and friend, AA carried me. When my father died in 2003, when my partner's mother lost her battle with cancer, when I went back to college, when I went through bad times at work, when my mother began to get old .... All the footprints in the sand left impressions I will never forget. So I strive to give back. In times of trial and suffering, when I thought I had to bear the weight myself, I am humbled and grateful that people in AA carried me.

A.W.

Oregon City, Oregon

CHAPTER SIX

Forming True Partnerships

————— ✳ —————

AA women on repairing, renewing and rethinking
romantic relationships

In the Big Book, the alcoholic is compared to "a tornado" running
through the lives of others, breaking hearts and ruining "sweet
relationships." As many alcoholics have discovered, this can
continue into sobriety. Learning how to live in "peace and partnership" with others is, as it says in our literature, a "moving and fascinating adventure." The sober women in this chapter recount their
experiences with relationships in sobriety.

In the story "Undue Influence," Jennifer R. meets a friendly guy in a
Big Book study who conceals bad intentions under the guise of fellowship. He succeeds in upending her life. Jennifer reaches out to an AA
friend, who helps her get her life back on track.

In "A Child of Woodstock," this 67-year-old lesbian finds friendship
in sobriety with her ex-husband so they can still be parents to the son
their marriage produced.

Christina E., in the story "Woman to Woman," writes about looking
for romance in early sobriety. Luckily, she gets advice from her wise
sponsor about finding romance in the rooms. "The odds are good, but
sometimes the goods are odd," her sponsor says. Single now, the writer
is happy to be "a whole woman—not half of a couple." Working the
program helps many alcoholics heal relationships.

A Woman of Dignity
May 1999

For me, drinking and negative sexual behavior went hand in hand, practically from the beginning. Early sexual abuse and drinking drove my sexual behavior. I was the queen of the one-night or three-month relationship. I didn't know that if I didn't pick up a drink, I wasn't likely to wind up in bed with someone I didn't know. I did much that I'm not proud of. I got pregnant during a blackout. I drank to enable my sexual behavior and to rid myself of any shame I felt.

When I stopped drinking, I started caring more about who I was. I wanted to behave with self-respect. But my patterns and my underlying causes were still there. A big turning point came after I spent the night with someone I really in my heart did not want to be with. After that night, I looked in the mirror, looked myself in the eye, and said, "I forgive you." That was the last time I was with someone I didn't want to be with.

Celibacy was critical for me in order to change my sexual behavior. I continued to get involved in relationships during my first year of not drinking, placing my sobriety in peril. But at some point I became willing to stop the relationship rollercoaster and was able to commit myself to celibacy. I was dedicated to it for almost two years: no flirting, no dating, no kissing. As I told someone who asked me out during this time, "I have to invest in myself."

During this period of celibacy, I learned a tremendous amount about myself. I felt feelings I had been blocking for more than 20 years. I discovered pain from my past that was greater than anything I'd ever imagined. Giving myself this time was a priceless gift. During these months I wrote my Fourth Step, did my Fifth Step, worked Steps Six and Seven, and began Steps Eight and Nine. I put the focus on me.

I'd always believed in the rightness of long-term monogamous relationships sanctified by a Higher Power, as was taught to me by my parents and my religion. Before AA, I was simply incapable of acting on this belief. I was terrified of intimacy. Sex was one thing, but an honest look at what a long-term commitment might mean gave me a tightness in my throat and a feeling that my skin was crawling. I asked for God's help with this and I received it.

Today I have been in a relationship for five years and was married two years ago. Every time I look at the ring on my hand, I see that my Higher Power has done for me what I could not do for myself. I met my partner in AA and ours is a sober relationship based on spiritual principles. The word gratitude, or any other word for that matter, does not begin to describe what I owe to God for allowing me this gift.

I often think of the Promises in relation to my past and present sex conduct. The hardest one for me to feel is the one which says, "We will not regret the past or wish to shut the door on it." I do have regret for my past conduct, "an honest regret for harm done," to myself and others. But I don't wish to shut the door on it. By leaving the door open to examining the past, I can help myself and others. When I can help another recovering woman in changing her sex conduct, I know that the Promise, "No matter how far down the scale we have gone, we can see how our experience can benefit others," is coming true in my life. I am a sober woman of dignity, living a life beyond my wildest dreams.

Anonymous

Grapevine Online Exclusive
Woman to Woman
March 2013

When I first came into AA, I did not like women and certainly didn't feel that I had any use for them. I didn't trust women either. I had been stabbed in the back too many times in my life.

When I found myself released from a community alternative

program and in need of a sponsor, I thought, Oh no. I decided that I was OK on my own for right now and a sponsor could wait. I had been locked up for the last nine months so I had more sobriety under my belt than I had ever had. I was attending a lot of meetings and was required to attend group counseling twice a week and individual counseling once a week, so I was "OK for the moment."

However, I realized I was no longer "OK" when a man entered the picture one month later. After my incarceration, I was hungry for male companionship. I also knew that relationships were not suggested during the first year of sobriety. More than anything, I knew that relationships had always been bad for me and I was headed for trouble. There were red flags popping up all around this man and this situation. I got scared—and I got busy looking for a sponsor.

I attended a Big Book study every Sunday evening in the town where I lived. The woman who moderated that meeting, Ruthie B., seemed real nice and she was funny—I liked anyone who could make me laugh. She was 15 years older than me and that was bad because older, more confident women scared me. They reminded me of my mother, who really frightened me.

Ruthie was full of confidence. She had been sober 15 years and I thought she was one heck of a woman. I really liked her, which is unusual for me. I decided to give it a shot and called her one morning to ask if she would sponsor me.

"Perfect timing!" she said. "I'm on my way to give my lead at the alcoholic clinic in Youngstown. Why don't you come hear my story and we'll go from there?"

We met at the clinic an hour later. I listened to her story and was captivated from the start. She's got a way with words and a great sense of humor. She also drank like I drank and the more I heard, the more I liked and admired this Ruthie B. When she began to speak of her journey in recovery, I was hooked. She quoted the Big Book, spoke of AA history, and preached the Twelve Steps as being the only way to recover.

Wow. I really liked this lady! We were going to get along just fine.

After the meeting, we went to lunch. There was a small group of us, a few old-timers and some of us "newbies." Ruthie said she would be delighted to sponsor me but she did have a couple of requirements: I had to call her every day until I had one year sober and I had to attend the Sunday Night Big Book Study until we went through the entire book one time.

That seemed easy enough, so I agreed. She asked if I had done the Steps and I told her I had while I was in that community program. We had a wonderful time that day, sharing food and fellowship. Before I knew it, two hours had passed and we were heading home. I now had a sponsor.

Sure enough, I became involved with the "red flag" man soon after getting my sponsor. When I asked Ruthie about relationships in the first year, she said, "The Big Book has no opinion on the matter and therefore, neither do I." Well, I took that statement and ran with it!

It took me approximately six weeks to realize there was something very wrong with this relationship. Al was in AA too and one of Ruthie's favorite quotes about finding romance in the rooms of AA is: "Your odds are good, but sometimes the goods are odd." She was so right. Al was so emotional and needy that I felt as if the very life was being drained from me. When I spoke to Ruthie about it, she said, "Al is using you, dear, just liked he used alcohol to keep from looking at himself. We alcoholics will use anything—food, sex, drugs, relationships—anything to take the focus off of self."

A little lightbulb came on in my head and I stopped her right there. I said, "Oh, my God, Ruthie. That's exactly what I am doing. I'm using him for the same reason!" All I got from Ruthie was a half smile and a well-placed, "Hmmm."

That was the beginning of the end of that romantic relationship. It took a long time and some desperate measures on both his and my part, but today I am not only free of the man, but free of the whole man-addiction.

I'm alone with myself for the first time in my life, and you know what? I'm OK with that today. I am a whole person, a whole woman—not half of a couple.

This didn't happen overnight. I went through some tough times getting to know myself and being comfortable with being alone. You've got to like yourself first, then come to know and love yourself for what you are, with all the good and all the bad that comes with it.

Through these experiences, I believe I learned why I hadn't liked being friends with women. It was because I hadn't liked myself.

Ruthie B. is still my personal angel, the most wonderful woman I have ever known. God knew exactly who to send as my teacher, and when to send her. I sponsor young women myself these days and nothing brings me more joy.

Christina E.
Newton Falls, Ohio

A Child of Woodstock
March 2009

I'm 67 years old, and this year I am working on my 21st year of sobriety in AA. I write these words and instantly think: How can I possibly be this old? How can I not have had a drink since December 1987? Well, the answer to the second question is obvious. And, come to think of it, probably the first: AA is how. My gratitude is boundless.

I was born and raised in Greenwich Village and Woodstock, New York, during the 40s and 50s, among artists and writers whose social lives were steeped in alcohol. During the day, they worked intensely at their art. Come evening, they got together and drank, intensely. The artists' parties were legendary, and since I was an only child and my parents had no money for babysitters, they brought me along. The artists got used to me, even adopted me. From the age of five on, I was a child of Woodstock. I felt that I was one of them.

My parents were both newspaper writers, and like their coworkers and their friends, they had learned to drink during Prohibition—

crazily, that is to say, as if the speakeasy were about to be raided at any minute. Theirs has been called the greatest generation, and growing up, I thought it was. I thought them wonderful, all these giants of my childhood. I still do. The only problem was I wanted to be just like them, in every way.

I began to drink with them in high school, tentatively. At dinner parties, I would have a glass of wine. I didn't really like wine, but I did like holding a wineglass in one hand and a mentholated cigarette in the other. It made me feel sophisticated. Then in the summer before college, in a town called Liberty, where I was working, I discovered Moscow Mules: vodka and ginger beer served in mule-shaped mugs. I liked Moscow Mules a whole lot better than wine, and that had very little to do with the mugs.

I went to college in a town where I could only order 3.2 beer until age 21. But there were parties to go to, given by grad students—especially chemistry department parties, where the punch consisted of fruit juice spiked with gallons of lab alcohol. By my sophomore year, I had begun to drink every weekend, every night, and even though I wasn't drinking to oblivion each time, I knew my friends weren't drinking half as often as I did, nor half as much. It scared me, even as I prided myself on being able to hold my liquor. On visits home, I loved to go to bars with Daddy and match him scotch for scotch. He was proud of me for being a chip off the old block. Yet I began to feel, whenever I thought about alcohol, the nameless dread I was to feel for years and never articulate to anyone, because I knew no one would know what I was talking about.

Years later, at my first AA meeting, I remember thinking, These people in this room would understand me if I mentioned my dread. I remember being swept with a relief as palpable as a martini in my veins.

But I had more than alcohol to dread. At 15, I had met an older woman—she was all of 20—and we'd fallen in love, although we didn't know that's what it was. We were as pure as the driven snow, and as naive. But my mother wasn't. She was full of fear and homophobia, which ruled back then, even (ironically) among her bohemian friends.

So to protect me from perversion, as she saw it, she put a stop to our communicating with each other. What a struggle it was to unlearn this behavior. Without AA, it would have been impossible.

Five years later, during my junior year abroad in Paris, where I was becoming a Great Writer (read: drinking as alcoholically as Hemingway), my teenage crush came after me, and we had an affair. Those were the days of "Pillow Talk," when women were supposed to fall in love with Rock Hudson, not Doris Day. I hated myself and demonized her, and stayed drunk most of that year in Europe. When I came home, I went into therapy.

I got cured. I got married to the closest approximation of Rock Hudson I could find. We had two children. Then, one night in the 10th year of our marriage, my husband confessed that he had been sleeping with men on the side for years.

What is relevant here, as I began to realize slowly in AA, is that it was alcohol that made our marriage possible for all the years we stayed together. We drank as our parents did, and liquor flowed into the fissures between us. It erased our reality. It cloaked our deep estrangement from each other and ourselves. It made deception and inauthenticity livable. And when my husband told the truth and my world collapsed, alcohol was my anesthesia. Drinking—drunk—I didn't have to feel so searingly what I was feeling. And so I got through 10 more years.

Until the day liquor stopped working. Suddenly, I could not count on it. I no longer knew what it would do to me. A pint of vodka sometimes went down like a pint of water. No effect at all. On a different day, a sip of vodka, or scotch, or wine, could send me staggering, my words slurred, my nose as red as Rudolph's. The only thing I could count on was that after I took my first drink, I couldn't stop. And from day to day, no matter how much booze I'd poured into the sink, first thing in the morning, promising myself that this was it, by late afternoon I couldn't not take my first drink. I'd go and buy another bottle.

It was a therapist who first suggested that I try AA. I was infuriated and offended, but that night I found a meeting. As soon as I walked in, I knew that I was home—even though I didn't yet believe I was an alcoholic and left the Fellowship at the end of six months. My excuse: It was just uncivilized not to drink a glass of wine with dinner.

Five years later, speaking of uncivilized, I was taking bottles of vodka to bed with me. I'd done Bill W.'s experiment with controlled drinking and he had proven his point.

The second time I came into AA, in 1987, it was my children who got me there, especially my son. A number of his friends in high school were abusing alcohol and drugs, and they had gone to meetings and reported to him he could meet girls there, so he'd gone along to an open meeting to see. When he got home, he said to me, "Man, there are some really weird characters at AA meetings!" And without thinking, I responded heatedly, "Those people are the salt of the earth! Those are among the bravest, kindest, smartest people I have ever met!" And I heard myself, and thought, What am I doing out here, away from them?

Twenty-one years later, my first years in the Fellowship are still vivid to me. Back then, everything that happened in my life called for a drink, which called for many more. Every pang of grief or guilt, every twinge of euphoria, every moment of boredom, every moment of excitement, each Thanksgiving, New Year's Eve, Memorial Day, work day, each day of the week was an occasion for drinking. What a struggle it was to unlearn this behavior, one day at a time, to reclaim my life, my consciousness, my self, and to accept that self. Without the Fellowship of AA, it would have been impossible.

Just one more thing: I think it's important to tell you that I am agnostic, and that the Higher Power—or, rather, the Greater Power—that has never let me down in these 21 years of sobriety, is Alcoholics Anonymous itself. I think it is crucial to say that you can get sober and stay sober and lead a wonderful life in AA without embracing a personal God. I don't believe in such a God; I do believe you have a perfect right to. I am not angry about anybody else's religious beliefs, I have no interest in changing them, I have no axe to grind. It troubles me sometimes when I am condescended to, in the Fellowship, for my own beliefs. But this is a small price to pay for the privilege of being sober and learning how to live. I believe in the astonishing power that emanates from a group of drunks helping each other, talking and listening to each other, with generosity and compassion and as much honesty as they can scrape together. I believe this life is all we have, and that fact renders it too precious to waste by drinking it away.

Today I have a loving partner and two loving grown-up children. My son, who joined AA a little over two years ago, asked me to speak on Mother's Day at the meeting he was chairing. I can think of no greater gift. He is now newly married and expecting a son of his own. My former husband and I walked him down the aisle together, in the upper meadow of what used to be my parents' house in Woodstock. I am filled with joy.

Nancy K.
Woodstock, New York

Falling Off the Sled
July 2007

My first sponsor asked me about what I felt when I walked into AA. The first time, I was at a meeting in Alaska that packed in more than 50 people. I was surrounded by a room full of vibrant, happy, sober people. All this Eskimo woman felt was loneliness and fear.

As a practicing alcoholic, I put myself in unhealthy situations. I married young to an alcoholic; by the time he was 23, he already had two DUIs. He mistreated me, fooled around and beat me. I spent five days in the hospital after one of his blackout rages. After 17 years, I left him.

One Christmas Eve, I had a gun held to my head by a boyfriend whom I would later marry. It wasn't unusual for the law to be called to defuse a confrontation between us, and in less than two years we would divorce. That was when I was introduced to AA by the Alaska Court System. But I wasn't only a victim. I was a volunteer.

I felt that my life had to change if I was going to develop healthy relationships. I had no self-worth, no self-respect, no dignity and very few friends. I had a boyfriend who brutally beat me two weeks after he broke up with me. I ended up in the hospital.

I was ignorant, in denial and full of resentment. I had a sponsor who didn't want to sponsor me because most court-ordered individuals rarely stay in AA, but she took me in because I was a suffering alcoholic. After six months of sobriety, I became willing and I began working the Steps. Part of my Step work was to reach deep into the recesses of my past and recall when it was that I felt overwhelming fear and loneliness and to put it on paper.

When I was about three years old, my family lived on the North Slope. We used to travel by dogsled during the tuberculosis epidemic in the late 1950s. During one trip, my mother and older brother were on the front of the sled as counterweight. There were supplies packed in the middle, and I sat below my father as he guided the dogs through the tundra. They stopped to watch a wolverine and I leaned over to look. When my father ordered the dogs to move forward, I tumbled out of the sled. The sled kept going, and my family looked smaller as distance grew between us. Fear and loneliness overwhelmed me.

My father came back to get me after my mother noticed that I was gone. He packed supplies around me to keep me secure. I cried and threw a fit because I could hardly move. I had a similar experience walking into AA; I was struggling, I cried and I threw fits because I couldn't drink. But the security of AA kept me safe, and packed enough AA into my head to keep me from falling off the wagon, or in my case, the dogsled.

In my first year of sobriety, I learned to develop a relationship with my Higher Power and I was blessed with a spiritual advisor who taught me how to meditate. I would recall sitting on the tundra with my grandmother, picking salmonberries, and she would always tell me to listen. Although I wasn't sure what she meant, she was actually teaching me how to listen to the wind and the earth; this was her way of meditation and prayer. It was similar to how my spiritual advisor taught me to meditate.

In AA I learned to be accountable for my actions. My spiritual advisor taught me to honor my relationships with everyone, and that meant everyone. This included my family, friends, coworkers and people in general. I learned that I am not responsible for other people's actions, including ex-husbands and boyfriends. I needed to continue to make a living amends to myself, my children and people from my past and present, even if I was never to see them again.

I learned not to let the past rule me, and I learned to let go of resentments from my past. I used to nurture my resentments until I was consumed, and it made me bitter. I wasn't going to develop healthy relationships if I didn't learn forgiveness. AA taught me how. Today, I have a happy, healthy relationship with my family. I have true friends and a wonderful mate. My sponsor told me that if I don't want to recapture the feeling of loneliness and fear, then remember when I fell off the dogsled.

Sarah J.
Boise, Idaho

Undue Influence
January 1993

On the first day I attended a Step and Big Book study group in my area, an extremely friendly guy named C. introduced himself to me. He was all smiles and very warm and welcoming. I decided to make this my home group since at one time I had been advised to attend a Step study group on a regular basis. I kept coming back to the meeting.

The following week, my new AA friend offered to give me rides to the meeting every week and treated me to dinner when our group met at a nearby restaurant an hour before the meeting. At first, I got a funny feeling in my gut, but I said to myself, Don't be paranoid!

He's just trying to reach out and be very welcoming. So I went along with this.

C. heard me comment at one of the meetings that I still got thoughts of drinking occasionally, even though I really didn't want to drink when it came right down to it. He came up to me after the meeting and said I needed to do another Fourth Step. I told him I was already working on a Fourth Step with my current sponsor of three-and-a-half years.

The following week, C. presented me with a guide of the "right" way to do a Fourth Step. He later told me he would like to sponsor me, to which I promptly replied, "Women should sponsor women and men should sponsor men." He said this didn't necessarily hold true at all times. I still felt this vague sense of unease, but he kept saying, "Don't worry, I'm not trying to get in your britches!" So I thought, Oh, what the heck! After all, he had been sober for eight years, he knew the Big Book like the back of his hand and he seemed to genuinely care. My current sponsor was out of town for long stretches 50 percent of the time, so I agreed to let C. co-sponsor me. However, I told him I would not discuss sex issues with him, as I would only discuss this with another woman. He promptly and enthusiastically tried to talk me into having a deeper trust in him. He said he hoped I could discuss anything with him, including sex.

My husband got wind of the fact that this man, a stranger to him, was escorting his wife to meetings, treating her to dinner, and wanting her to discuss our intimate life with him. My husband blew up, of course. I then called my new male sponsor and told him about my husband's angry explosion. C. said he couldn't see how I could stay sober with a spouse like that, and asked if he should come over. I said, "No!" quite emphatically. Several days later C. told me that he wanted to come to my home so he could pick me up and take me to a shelter for recovering women alcoholics to get me away from this "abusive" husband of mine. At first, I was angry at my husband for blowing up. One of my shortcomings was being naive. I went along with C. I agreed that my husband was being abusive and wondered what to do about it.

Several days later, after much upheaval, I consulted an old and trusted friend in the program about all this. My friend helped me realize that my original unease was well-founded. I realized—albeit rather belatedly—that this character C. was definitely performing a masterminded "thirteenth step" on me! Right away, I terminated my relationship with C. completely. I stopped blaming my spouse for being as furious as he was, and was reassured that in fact he had been treating me quite well all along.

After all this happened, I was very tempted to take out the whip and give myself a good beating for being so dumb! But my friends in AA said, "Don't be too hard on yourself." I put the whip away and focused instead on being grateful for the fact that things had gone no further than they had.

I hope newcomers and old-timers alike will take heed and listen to some advice: 1) Women, get a female sponsor. Men, get a male sponsor. 2) Lean on your Higher Power; don't lean on another member of AA too heavily. We all have clay feet—i.e., we are not perfect.

As Tradition Five states, "Each group has but one primary purpose—to carry its message to the alcoholic who still suffers." AA is not a place to try to pick up members of the opposite sex.

Tradition Two says that "there is but one ultimate authority—a loving God as He may express Himself in our group conscience. Our leaders are but trusted servants; they do not govern." So one AA member can't be an authority over any other member. Even a good sponsor can only give guidance and helpful advice. No member of AA should ever tell another member to break up a marriage.

And just as each AA group ought to be fully self-supporting, I believe that I as an AA member ought to fully support myself and my endeavors when I can afford it, declining outside contributions.

Well, this experience has sure taught me a couple of lessons! By passing on my experience, I hope that others will avoid this same problem—especially newcomers. After all, I want them to keep coming back!

Jennifer R.
St. Louis, Missouri

Grapevine Online Exclusive

A Portrait of a Marriage

May 2015

The morning George and I got married in 1965 in Lenox, Massachusetts, I had a fierce hangover and wanted a drink really badly. We only invited George's family to celebrate with us. We were married by a Justice of the Peace who was also a pig farmer. He lived right next door to a motel, so we planned on staying there the night of our wedding.

After the ceremony, we went to the motel. However, the wind was blowing the wrong way and the smell from the pig farm was overwhelming. We had some drinks but even that could not dull the smell. We drove to Amenia, Connecticut, which was a dry town after midnight. We managed to get some booze before the witching hour came.

The next morning we drove to Hollywood, Florida. We spent the time drinking, swimming, eating out and drinking some more. We thought we were having a grand time.

A few years later, I got sober. George didn't at the time but he came around several years later, in 1974. We had a hell of a time trying to hold our marriage together. We even went to see a lawyer about dissolving it.

I felt like I no longer knew who George was and I was filled with fear that he would not like me sober—after all, we had met in a bar. I didn't know if I still even liked him. After he stopped drinking, I spent a couple of years hitting him over the head with AA literature, trying to get him to work the program the way I did. But he was his own man and wouldn't do as I said.

He did attend meetings, which actually scared me because I saw them as my meetings and I worried that someone might tell him of things I had said about him. People suggested to me that George and

I attend different meetings. At first I resented this, but I followed the suggestion.

George and I grew apart for a period of time. His son, my stepson, came back into our lives and that brought us back together. We had two children of our own by this point as well. George and I decided to move in the hopes that a change of scene might help us renew our relationship. That helped a lot.

Over many years, we struggled though much dysfunctional thinking and feelings. We both had to learn how to let go of yesterdays.

God was good to me to bring George into my life, regardless of the struggles we have had. No one knows me better than he does. He had a lot of patience and tolerance as I got sober and went through many changes. Neither of us doubt that God did for us what we could not do for each other.

Today we have a wonderful friendship, a deep love—the kind that comes from sharing a lifetime with each other. We have shared the good and the bad, the happy and sad. We have grown up together. We are two different people and within our marriage, we are still learning how to put principles before personalities. Neither of us is perfect but we are enjoying the journey together.

Lee G.
Tabernacle, New Jersey

CHAPTER SEVEN

Our Families

———— ✳ ————

Sober women heal and grow in their relationships with
their children, partners and parents

Many alcoholics suffer most from "twisted relations" with family, so writes our co-founder Bill W. in the "Twelve and Twelve." In the following chapter, AA women share their experiences in healing the past and navigating family relationships sober in the present.

Angry with her teenage son and out of answers, Doni H., in her story, "Energy Generation," tries out a new meeting, where she finds a room full of alcoholic teens who have plenty of experience, strength and hope to share.

In "When Every Meeting Counts," a member becomes a mother for the first time, putting her eight years of sobriety to the test.

In "In All the Wrong Places," Heidi R. finds a love and acceptance at her AA meeting place, something which seemed absent from her family growing up.

Sheila O., in "A Glimpse Through the Window," finally realizes the full effect of her sobriety on her family from the smile on her husband's face. He tells her that now he's happy to come home from work every day.

When it comes to our family relationships, these stories share a common theme: There is reason to have hope.

When Every Meeting Counts
June 2001

Like most of us, I consider my biggest life-changing event to be the day I walked into an AA meeting. So I was not at all prepared for the metamorphosis I underwent with the birth of my daughter eight sober years later.

Before this event, I had a wonderful husband with 17 years of sobriety, a sponsor, a home group and a support network of AA friends. I was reaping the joys of sobriety: a normal life and sometimes even one with serenity and stability.

But I was unprepared to deal with the 24-hour-a-day demands of an infant: no sleep, no meetings, and barely enough time to talk with my sponsor. Though never hungry, I was constantly lonely and tired, and as a result, irritable, discontent and angry.

One night, in tears and frustration, I sat rocking my daughter and asked my husband, "Why didn't you tell me it was going to be this hard?" (God only knows the love this man has shown for me in being willing to undertake another child in midlife. As my youngest stepchild becomes a senior in high school, our daughter will enter kindergarten.)

With so many diaper changes in my life, my sober friendships eventually became strained. Consumed with my child, I couldn't relate to the freedom and problems of my childless friends. I craved the companionship of other mothers, sitting in AA or strolling down the street of my neighborhood. The isolation of having a baby was very painful to me.

"Keep It Simple" became my basic level of functioning. Since I was no longer able to get to a meeting when I needed or wanted one, every meeting counted. I had a very erratic work schedule and finding babysitters proved to be daunting. At first, I took my daugh-

ter to my home group with some regularity, but it was difficult to con-
centrate, wondering if at any moment she would cry. As she got older
and started to toddle around, I sat at the back of the room, straining
to hear. I was grateful to be in the spirit of the meeting, but I was
barely hanging on. I suggested we offer babysitting at the meeting,
but this met with lukewarm support. I just didn't have the resources
to find a regular sitter at the time. Some members were supportive;
others let me know quite clearly how upset they were that my baby
was interrupting their sharing.

I left my home group in frustration. A new solution presented itself
when my husband found an early morning Saturday meeting. Often
leaving home in darkness, we attended regularly while my stepdaugh-
ter stayed with the baby. This small meeting with intimate sharing
became my lifeline for two years. Topics focused on recovery from alcoholism, and my sobriety was strengthened by the love and support
I received there.

Recently, I started a meeting at my daughter's preschool. We meet
while her class is in session, so I don't have to find a babysitter. I enjoy the responsibility and commitment of setting up this meeting as
much as I did my first years of sobriety. As my meetings are fewer, I
need to hear topics grounded in AA each week, so we always read a
topic from our literature. Once, when no one showed up, I decided
to read the Third Step from the "Twelve and Twelve." I was so taken
by how many times the word "willingness" appeared that it led me
to a study of the entire "Twelve and Twelve." Then I went back to the
Big Book and joined an online Big Book study group. Our literature
is vital to my path in sobriety now. My prayer life has also deepened.
Regular prayer and outside support are great comforts. These are
tools I learned in AA.

Since having my daughter, I have learned much from my husband
and my sponsor about self-sacrifice. For someone used to living life in
the driver's seat, even in sobriety, this was a rude awakening. Having
a child is utterly humbling. I write this to offer hope and encouragement to other sober new mothers. Too often I have seen women in AA

leave the Fellowship as the demands of their children and families take over. Prayer and a willing heart enabled me to find what I needed to stay sober and connected to the Fellowship. It is not easy, but it is entirely worth it.

Looking back, I am so grateful for the motivation of my "new life challenges." My daughter continually makes me work on myself to become a healthy mother, and this in turn strengthens my sobriety.

M.S.W.
Richmond, Virginia

In All the Wrong Places
August 2000

I was brought up in a household where children were to be seen and not heard. Alcohol was seldom present in our home, apart from the few liquor-filled chocolates my mother would treat herself to from time to time.

My father's role was that of disciplinarian and breadwinner. We all feared his anger. When we were punished, it was usually physical. I don't remember the words "I love you" said out loud in the home. I never once, as a child, saw my father hug or kiss my mother.

Usually after a physical episode, my father would come to my bed at night. He would tell me that he loved me and that he touched me the way that he did because I was his "special girl." As a child who desperately wanted his love and approval, I believed him. I did not feel it was wrong at the time.

When I was 11 or 12 years old, my dad found religion. He became fully absorbed in the church, and our "special times" stopped. I felt abandoned and hated God for taking my dad away from me. I decided to give church a try in the hope that it would please my father. When it was apparent to me that church came first (as we were told many times), I started to rebel. At age 13, I picked up my first drink.

I was thrilled at how good it made me feel. I thought I had found the answer to my broken heart. I was invited to my first party with the "in crowd." I was ecstatic that I finally was being accepted and became extremely drunk for the first time. Three of the boys decided to take advantage of my situation. You can well imagine the rest.

I woke up the next morning feeling very ashamed, but most of all, very angry. Although the "special times" had ceased with my father, the physical discipline hadn't. He beat me for the condition I had come home in. By this time, I knew that what he had done to me as a child was wrong. With every blow that day, my anger and resentment grew.

I ran away many times, and at age 15, I finally ran away for good.

The next few years I led an extremely self-destructive life. Alcohol and drugs were my constant companions. I married three times, always to men who were just a little sicker than I was, and I ran away from all three of these marriages. In the meantime, I had two children from my second marriage and two more children from my third.

I have been down many roads in my years of drinking. I tried prostitution and lesbianism. I ran with a prominent bike club for a couple of years. In essence, I see now that I was looking for love in all the wrong places.

I was nowhere near ready to be a mom when I had my children. But somehow, I did manage to instill in all of them a sense of love and being loved. How I did that I do not know because they spent most of their younger years (especially my two older boys) with sitters and in day care. All I know is that I didn't let a day go by without telling them that I loved them. The same applies today.

I met a young woman when I was 18 years old who was everything I wanted to be. She was your typical motorcycle mama. We partied together for many years, but about the time that I was getting married for the third time, she got sober. I was very angry, and the old feelings of being abandoned by someone I loved surfaced again.

Over the next few years, my drinking accelerated to a new level. I became secretive and started hiding my booze and drugs from my children. Then one Christmas, I ended up in a hospital, where my gall-bladder was removed. My doctor asked me how much I drank. When I tried to tell him that I was an occasional drinker, he said that I might be able to fool some people. I might even be able to fool myself, but pictures don't lie. He said that my liver was showing signs of infection, and if I didn't change my drinking habits, I would not be around to see my daughters grow up. (I was only 36 years old.)

My husband asked me if I would give our marriage one more try. As I was living in a one-and-a-half-bedroom trailer with three of my children, I said yes. We moved out in the country near Delhi, Ontario. Not long after, we split up for the last time. My best friend started coming around, and I was amazed at the change in her. She had managed to stay sober for nine-and-a-half years and was very active in AA. Through her gentle persuasion, I began to take care of myself physically. For instance, for many years I had been living with a 70 percent hearing loss, which I didn't care about when I was drinking. She drove me to many appointments with doctors, and I now have hearing aids.

Finally, I decided that I was pretty tired of being sick all the time and began going to a few meetings with her. I had a real hard time with the God concept, as I had spent most of my life blaming God for everything that went wrong. To help, my friend talked me into going with my kids to an AA campout, where I got a good dose of spirituality. However, I didn't know how to deal with these feelings yet, so with 60 days of sobriety under my belt, I ran.

I spent the next few months trying to prove (once again) that I could drink normally. Then, a week before Christmas, I went to a party, where I started power-drinking tequila and smoking marijuana. I ended up spending most of the night hanging out the door of a pickup truck. For the first time, I noticed blood in my vomit. A few days later, as I found myself sitting in a restaurant with my second beer in front of me, I realized that my life had become unmanageable and I was powerless over alcohol. I haven't had a drink since. I'm not running anymore.

I spent that Christmas with my best friend in Hamilton, Ontario, at a club of alcoholics. The club stayed open around the clock for three days over the Christmas holidays, and groups from surrounding areas took turns putting on meetings.

It was an amazing time. In all my experiences at church, I had never felt the presence of God as strongly as I did at that hall. People from all over donated food and paper plates, so we were able to keep a table of food full throughout the event. We were also able to fill the hall for a fabulous sit-down turkey dinner. The unconditional love and caring that was put forth in that room was overwhelming.

On the final day, my home group from Delhi walked in. It was their turn to put on the meeting. I was surprised at the way they talked and accepted me as a part of the group, as if I had never left. Even though I had hidden in the kitchen during most of the other meetings, this time I found myself at the front of the room, reading the Twelve Steps. I have been on the road to recovery ever since.

It's not always easy. Some days it is downright difficult. The big difference this time is that I'm not going it alone. I truly believe that with the help of my Higher Power, all things are possible.

This weekend, I am putting on an Easter dinner. All my children will be together, and my parents will be here too. I will never be able to forget what my father did to me as a child, but I have been able to forgive him. He is not the same man that he was all those years ago.

This is one of the many rewards of staying sober. It could never have happened without the support of my home group and a couple of very special friends.

Heidi R.
Delhi, Ontario

Energy Generation
October 1989

W hen I was newly sober, I couldn't figure out why people with years of sobriety drank again. When I was sober for six years I began to have a little understanding about that mystery because it almost happened to me.

Once in a while my self-will runs wild, but I've been more of an observer of life rather than a participant; a serious, afraid-to-take-risks person living in fantasy. Before I stopped drinking I could picture what I wanted and that seemed good enough. I thought I was having all the benefits with none of the work. AA has helped me live more and fantasize less, yet I secretly felt that if things got really bad I could always drink again.

Coming so close to a drink six years ago forced me to join up with life, to take it on its own terms, not mine, to not take failure so seriously and to take a few risks. Like it says in Step Ten: maintain my sobriety under all conditions, in fair weather or foul.

The last three years have been much better, much happier, except for the problems I've been having with my son. Since last summer we've both gotten worse. Although I've been sharing with my sponsor, a shrink and two probation counselors, I've gradually slipped back into that terrible victim place where I cry, I protest, I blame and nothing changes. I took a week off from work and stayed in bed.

AA people have helped me and loved me many times these past nine years, but last night was so special—last night my Higher Power brought me into the presence of angels.

Yesterday afternoon I was angry about my son. I shared my pain in a large, crowded group of recovering alcoholics and only one man responded. "Yeah, motherhood is tough," he said. I went back to work with red eyes, feeling wild because I'd made a fool out of myself again.

Feeling sick of being me, I wanted to run away to a place where no one knew me, where I could get a new start. Maybe I could even run away and after a while, have just one drink,

That evening I drove home, didn't cook, smoked a lot of cigarettes, felt the incredible bondage that only an alcoholic can feel, and finally it was time to go to a meeting. I had heard there was a new Step meeting nearby that needed support, and I knew I needed another meeting, so off I went. I was early, and only a few young people were there. Every time the door opened more young people came in. Pretty soon the room was full of youngsters. Everyone there looked close to 17—my son's age. I wanted to run away. I thought this was going to be a small meeting! The Preamble was read, reports were given by the treasurer and GSR, and then Step One was read. I heard the words, "liberation and strength." That's what I could hope for. My hand was the first one raised.

I told them how it was, that this kid of mine was my favorite. I told them what was happening at home. I wanted them to know about me—that I was the kind of person who would rather burn down my house than clean my bedroom, that I'm either Chicken Little or a raving maniac. I told them I couldn't take the fights we were having and yet I couldn't stand being bullied when I pretended everything was OK. "My son is in trouble with drugs," I told them. "He hates the world and refuses to be a part of it. My shrink says I have to be strong, but the sadness and guilt are tearing me apart."

I saw a lot of hands go up. I didn't know what to expect from them. As these kids talked to me something started to happen. It was like sitting inside a generator of energy. They hadn't tuned me out—they cared. They spoke to me about family memories that caused them pain and they spoke in spite of their own pain. I could see by their faces they were paying a heavy price to talk to me, to tell me how it was with them and how it is now. I saw at least 30 angels in different clothing and different hairstyles with the same light shining inside. It was courage and responsibility. I was looking at the pain and the light of courage. I was looking at kids with God's love inside.

The meeting was over. Do you think they stopped? No way. There were more discussions, more energy, more support, more ideas, hugs, telephone numbers, even a written list of "house rules" placed in my hands. I was invited to go to the diner and another band of AA rein-forcements were waiting for me. This time the table seated men and women almost as old as me. After more support I rejoined two of my cherubs in a nearby booth and as we shared and laughed I told them I was still 19 inside.

This morning I woke up a different person. I'm a better, stronger person because of those kids. I have seen courage, sensed courage in the rooms of AA, but last night I looked into its face.

Doni H.
Fairfield, Connecticut

A Compelling Angel
August 2000

Toward the end of my 20 years of drinking, I was a tired, iso-lated hausfrau, caring for a beautiful year-old boy—after a fashion—and continuing my quest to drink all day and in secret, to escape detection and disapproval from my husband. I idly wondered how long I could get away with it. Even though my husband hadn't uncovered the hard evidence yet, I already was paying a stiff price. I stubbornly ignored spiritual bankruptcy, sluggishness and growing medical evidence of liver problems, which I blamed on other factors, so I could muddle on with my daily quart of vodka habit. I spent a frightening amount of time, energy and effort in maintaining my secret boozing, which didn't show up as messy drunkenness, but as bloat, laziness and irresponsibility—on a good day.

Despite what now seem like clear and present dangers, I told my-self that I would keep drinking until I got caught, figuring that had to happen at some point. The prospects were scary, but at the time, not drinking was not an option. I was sipping all day and all night, drinking solo, or, when in the company of others, managing frequent bathroom trips accompanied at all times by my bottle-heavy purse. The daily quart had long since ceased to be a source of pleasure or euphoria. I needed to get out of bed and deal with the day, however badly. I knew from past experience that withdrawal seizures were inevitable if I stopped suddenly, and cutting back was hardly an option.

The only witness to my endless boozing was my son who, I consoled myself, wouldn't "tell" because he couldn't even talk! But my soul would shrivel up when I noticed his preoccupation with the bottles he saw being poured all day long. He was always reaching for them, touching them, removing them from my purse, playing with them like sinister toys. But even this didn't spur me into action. I hoped against hope the bottles wouldn't remain in his memory for long. Then I dismissed the whole sordid, pathetic image from my mind.

What I didn't know was that he was the one who would eventually "rat me out." Toward the end of my drinking, I was getting more and more careless with the location of my pocketbook, which I joked to myself was my portable bar. Time passed, and my husband grew enormously quiet and distant. He appeared to be carrying a burden of grief that he wouldn't discuss, and his silence and detachment finally began to penetrate my fog. I begged him to tell me what was wrong, and received monosyllables for answers, until one day he painfully said, "Why don't you tell me about what you've been carrying around in your pocketbook?" My first knee-jerk, denial-ridden reaction was, "What have you been doing—going through my pocketbook?" Despite the unbelievable insensitivity of my remark under the circumstances, my husband assured me he hadn't been snooping; it was in fact our son, who at every opportunity had opened my purse, showing my husband the contents. My husband had not only seen the bottles, but seen that the bottles changed brands and emptiness levels daily. He was baffled and disgusted by the volume of my drinking, but almost destroyed by the fact that I had hidden it and lied about it.

Around this time, sorrowful, guilty and eager to make some sort of amends, I went to my first meeting of Alcoholics Anonymous. I walked in knowing I was an alcoholic; I had that much awareness. But the once-successfully secretive nature of my drinking had led me to believe that I could continue to drink, as long as I put a decent face on it. Never mind that I was sick in soul and body. Never mind that I was a neglectful mom who spent the day drinking endlessly while my son slept. Never mind that I was poisoning myself. Never mind that I was risking the life I valued and that I wanted to stay with my husband and little boy, because I refused to confess my alcoholism and seek help. I was at a pitiful impasse.

So my son, just over a year old at the time, kept blowing the whistle on his mom. He brought my husband to a vodka-soaked shirt that I'd put in his hamper. He kept revealing the contents of my pocketbook until my husband started checking it himself—always, but always, finding evidence. Finally, my son forced my hand. I had to walk into an AA meeting room in order, I thought, to show my good intentions and save my marriage.

A little over two years later, after facing my disease and my responsibility to tackle it a day at a time, I am a relieved, astounded and joyful sober wife, mom and woman. With time, effort and grace, I've regained my husband's trust. Not being an alcoholic himself, he's inclined to write off this whole painful time as an unfortunate lapse of judgment. He probably wouldn't even mind my not going to meetings anymore. But I know better. And in fact, he facilitates my getting to daily meetings and doesn't talk about it much. This system allows me to stay sober on my own terms and accept his confusion and reticence about the matter. So far, it serves us both well. But no matter how he reacts, I now know I have to work the program for the rest of my life—one day at a time.

None of this would have come about had it not been for my little boy who, in his inarticulate, baby-like way, did what he could to stop what he must have intuited was his mom's self-destruction. I believe God often works through the people in our lives. He sure picked a compelling little angel to come to my assistance. I'm very grateful to my little guy, who is today a happy, goofy, affectionate three-year-old. He eased along the miracle and helped me when I was unable to help myself.

Ellen F.
New York, New York

Left-Handed
April 2007

"What was he like? What did he do?" I was stuck on the stepfather portion of my Fourth Step and my sponsor was drawing me out. A dozen years of descent into alcoholism brought me to AA at age 32. I was so desperate never to be compelled to drink again that I'd survived three years of Third Step struggle before caving in to a Greater Power. It was time to do the Fourth and Fifth, the elder statesmen said, or I would surely have to drink again.

I thought the portion about my mother would be the greatest problem in my searching and fearless inventory, but we'd handled that. My mother did the best she could with what she had to work with, we'd decided, and I had made the comparison and forgiven myself for the neglect of my own children. But there I was, unable to reconcile my resentment about my wicked stepfather.

"He was left-handed, like me," I blurted out. "And I hated it!" I went on to tell of his cruelties, of my hatred and how it had affected my life. Born in the last decade of the 19th century, the 60-year-old man knew only one method of discipline. He beat me, the precocious weird kid, for every real or imagined nonconformity—with belts and yardsticks and climbing boots.

Fourth Step or no Fourth Step, I would always hate him and that was that.

My sponsor didn't quit prodding me to get to the bottom of the resentment though, and the unconditional love I had come to know in Alcoholics Anonymous helped me to see the inhumanity of my last interaction with him, many years before. "Home" between husbands, I spelled my mother at his deathbed. He had no breath to speak, but his mouth formed a word, over and over again.

"Sorry. Sorry." His eyes pleaded with me on that August day in 1954, but I turned my back deliberately, unwilling to allow him a dying repentance. Now, the shame of that heartlessness was tearing me up.

At the Ninth Step, I followed my sponsor's instructions and wrote a stilted letter. "I'm mortally sorry," I wrote, "that I turned my back on your apologies. Today I would not do that." It was all I could do, and I still hated him as I burned the letter in the fireplace.

Nevertheless, my life settled into a semblance of normalcy as I practiced living in Steps Ten, Eleven and Twelve, experiencing exquisite tastes of happiness, joy and freedom in spite of myself and my lingering resentment. A couple of years later, a secretary brought me some papers to sign. "You write so beautifully," she exclaimed. "Most left-handers write upside down, or illegibly, or both."

I started one of the tragicomic tales about my childhood, how as a teenager my stepfather had made me write for an hour after school when I began to learn cursive writing, and for two hours during the summer. I was going to tell her how he'd rip up what I'd copied from storybooks if it didn't satisfy him and make me do it over again, and finish the story by joking that I had at least reaped a benefit from the torture. But I choked up and couldn't continue.

A thought appeared out of the blue. He wanted me to have better than he did. He was ashamed that he couldn't write. But he had done the best he could, with what he had to work with. Serenity filled me—great and warm and peaceful.

My last Ninth Step letter was written that night. "Thank you for my fine handwriting," it read. "I'm sorry for my years of hatred." Those years vanished up the chimney with the smoke as the page charred and burned.

That resentment has never wasted another precious moment of my new life, thanks to the Steps of Alcoholics Anonymous.

Judith N.
Marysville, Washington

Grapevine Online Exclusive
A Glimpse Through the Window
September 2011

I never fully realized the extent to which my drinking affected my family, until I was given a small glimpse from my husband one afternoon through a window.

My last year of drinking was a continued downward spiral into that black hole at the bottom of a bottle that many of us end up in. I had become a daily blackout drinker, and so much of what happened was told to me by my husband, daughters, family and friends, usually the next day after coming to.

I have no reason to doubt any of it, and know in my heart they have never been able to tell me all of it, and for that I am grateful. I learned once I got here that it didn't matter how long I drank, how much I drank, or what I drank ... what mattered is what happened every time I drank and that I couldn't stop.

I found AA and sobriety in September of 2002. With the help of the Fellowship, sponsors and my Higher Power, I haven't found it necessary to pick up a drink since that time. On my last day of drinking, I'd been told by my husband of more than 20 years that I needed to leave. He no longer could stand by and watch me tear apart our family; I was out of control, and the nightmare had to end for him and my two daughters who were 12 and 14 years old.

The next day I was admitted to a local detox, and that's where I first heard the message of hope that AA carries. Faced with the reality of losing my husband, children, home and sanity, I was given the gift of desperation. There were AAs who came to the detox each day who shared their experience, strength and hope with us. Thank God, my ears were open and I heard what I needed to. I identified with every speaker who shared ... all were telling my story.

Alcohol eventually took control of their lives, made them do things they never thought they'd do, say things they'd never thought they'd say, and become someone they never thought they'd be. They all spoke of ending in a hole at the bottom of a bottle, filled with guilt, shame, remorse, isolation, anger, despair, confusion, not knowing how they got there, and the total hopelessness of not knowing how to get out.

Then they each shared of somehow finding their way to AA, learning and using all that is offered there, and how their lives started to change. They told of being able to stay away from one drink, for one day, with the help of the Fellowship, sponsorship, joining a group and asking for help. Listening to each one of them, I finally knew I was an alcoholic, that I'd never be able to stop drinking on my own, and truly believed they had something I wanted and needed.

I jumped in with both feet, took suggestions, got a sponsor, joined a group and got active. I was walked through the Steps, and as promised, my life got better. Things started to slowly change, and I found myself not drinking, day after day.

I was riding on that pink cloud we hear about, and working my way through the wreckage. I was very fortunate in that I was able to come back to my home from that detox, and gradually things got better with my husband, children and family.

In early spring, a year and a half after I had finally put the drink down, I was standing at my kitchen sink doing dishes. We have a small window over the sink which looks out onto the front yard. My husband had just gotten home from work, and as he was coming up the walkway to the front door, he saw me in the window at the sink, and gave me the most beautiful smile.

As soon as he came through the door, I gave him a kiss on the cheek, and asked what the big smile was for. Yes, I was fishing for a compliment, the old pat on the back, of how glad he was to see me, or just how happy I make him. Fortunately, my Higher Power takes care of my ego on a regular basis, reminds me of who and where I am, and gives me just what I need to hear.

My husband kissed me back and said, "I just realized when I saw you in the window that I don't get sick coming home anymore." This was definitely not what I was expecting to hear. I asked him what he meant, "don't get sick?" He explained that every single day, for more than a year before I finally got sober until now, he would get in his truck to come home from work. By the time he hit the highway, his stomach would start to cramp a little and a headache would start.

By the time he got to our exit off that highway, his stomach would be in full rumble and his heart would be starting to race a little. By the time he pulled into our driveway, a cold sweat and nausea would be added. He never knew, every single day, what he would find on the other side of the door. Were his daughters OK? Was his wife passed out—again? Was she even home? Was she out there somewhere driving drunk with his girls in the car? Had she burned down the house? Had she gained access to the last bank account and the last of their money?

On my last day drinking, my husband, to end the nightmare, had to tell me to leave. Through the miracle of AA and learning not to drink one day at a time, this Fellowship has also given recovery to my husband, my family and my friends. I may have known in my heart as soon as I got here that I was done drinking for good, but for those who lived at the bottom of the bottle with me, it took a whole lot longer to believe it.

A hard lesson to hear. When I thought I wasn't hurting anyone else with my drinking, I was greatly mistaken. What a beautiful lesson to live. Sobriety heals more than just me, one day at a time.

Sheila O.

CHAPTER EIGHT

Worker Among Workers

———— * ————

Sober women in the workplace

T he stories in the following chapter show AA women reviving old dreams or making new ones, finding courage in sobriety instead of a bottle to pursue them, and equally important, simply learning to hold down a job.

Romey P., in the article "List of Dreams," goes back to school in sobriety and writes how she's "now doing things I'd only fantasized about when I had a vodka and tonic in one hand and my dream list in the other."

Patty G., in "Office Confidential," makes a sober friend at her job, a woman with the same name and sobriety date. She finds the AA love and support in the workplace that she knew from meetings.

In "Whatever It Takes," Lori T. takes the stage to recite her poetry, no longer having to down 18 ounces of straight scotch in order to do it.

In the story "Pandora's Bottle," M.C. tells about her "smarty-pants" job that drove her to drink. Now sober, she decides to pursue something less demanding, leaving more time for other meaningful things in life.

List of Dreams
August 2004

"I am 40 years old, I work in an hourly-wage job, and I have no husband to support me. I'm too old to go back to school. I'd be almost 50 when I would start a new career. I'm sober, but I still resent alcohol ruining my life!" So said an attractive, articulate woman at a meeting my husband and I attended on one of our adventures across the country.

I wanted to share an experience and some hope with this lady, but the meeting ended and she left hurriedly after the Lord's Prayer. What she had said was very similar to what I had said 14 years ago, at the age of 40. I also remember with brilliant clarity what was said to me: "Well, in 10 years you'll be 50 whether you go to school or not. Would you rather be 50 with a degree, or 50 without a degree?"

Now 54, I have had my PhD for two years. I worked full time, finished my undergraduate degree, and was accepted into a master's degree program the following year. The month I started graduate school, I was diagnosed with cancer (my past consumption of alcohol and withdrawals were primary factors). I had surgery and two and a half months of daily radiation. After three weeks off for surgery, somehow I continued to go to school and to work and completed that semester. My master's took me two years to complete; then I completed my doctoral program in a little over three years.

True, I'll probably be paying off my student loans with my social security checks, but that's OK. The years in school were some of the best in my 14 years of sobriety. I am now doing things I'd only fantasized about when I had a vodka and tonic in one hand and my dream list in the other.

One of my jobs is as an adjunct faculty member at a local university. I often hear women in their 30s and 40s use age as an excuse for not going to graduate school. If age is the only excuse, I tell them, they might want to reconsider.

Had I not remained sober, I would never have accomplished my goals. Remaining sober and following the principles I learned in AA allowed me to experience miracles beyond sobriety but not beyond my dreams. In sobriety, my dreams really do mean something.

Somewhere, I hope a woman in her 40s is reading this—and reconsidering her options.

Romey P.
Jeffersonville, Indiana

Office Confidential
January 2015

In early 1992, after working for the same government agency for over 20 years, I began a new career. Needless to say, I was very nervous in a new agency, in an entirely new city. Change was difficult for me.

On that first day of my new job, I found a deli across the street where I could buy lunch. As I stood on line waiting to order, I looked around and all I saw were shelves stacked with alcohol. I was surprised that seeing those bottles upset me so, since I had five years of sobriety. I immediately decided I needed to increase my meeting attendance to deal with this change. I reached for my meeting book in my desk drawer to find a nearby AA meeting. I still believe that the meeting book is the most necessary book in Alcoholics Anonymous.

I flipped through the book and found a women's meeting at noon near my office. Great, I thought, I'll go there tomorrow on my lunch hour. Then it dawned on me that I was unfamiliar with the area and had no inkling how to get there. I saw my colleague from the adjacent office pass by and called out to her. "Excuse me," I said, "do you know where Overlook Road is?" She stopped, stepped inside my office and closed the door. "I know exactly where it is," she said. "Are you going to a meeting?" I was flabbergasted. How did she know? I was shocked. This nice-looking, well-dressed woman with the faint fragrance of perfume was standing in my office telling me she was in the program? She then told me that there was only one building on Overlook Road, the temple where AA meetings were held. Once again, God was there for me.

After getting to know her better, we discovered that in addition to having the same name, we were the same age, and had the same sobriety date: April 22. I got sober in 1987, and she a year later. Throughout my years of working with her, we became dear friends and always marveled how we never went "off the AA beam" on the same day. We were always there for each other, offering a shoulder, a suggestion, or just to listen on those down days we would experience from time to time.

"You have to give it away to keep it," is a saying we both learned early in sobriety. We began a tradition: I passed my medallion to her the day of my anniversary, and we celebrated by going out to lunch or dinner. When I handed her my medallion, I would tell her what kind of a year I had and how my sobriety had helped me grow. Some years when we were too busy to celebrate with a meal together, we'd go across the street to the park for 10 minutes, sit on a bench, and continue our tradition.

The "God-incidence" of meeting my friend was so life-changing for me. Because of her generosity, she offered her winter home in southwest Florida in May 1993, so my husband and I could celebrate our first wedding anniversary. We fell so in love with the area that we purchased a small condo where we vacationed for years, making new friends at each meeting we attended during our vacations. With the encouragement of those new friends, we packed up and moved to southwest Florida in 2004. Our new life there is like living in our own Shangri-La.

I continue to pass my medallion to my dear friend every April 22 by mail, with a note about my sober life during the past year. We keep in touch, and I visit her when I go north to see my family. I miss my friend dearly, but know that we are together in spirit daily.

Whenever I am at the jumping off point, God steps in to rescue me.

I have experienced many "God-incidences" over the years, in all areas of my life. I know I'm never alone and, if I just let go, my God steps in and shows me the way. Finding my lifelong cherished friend was no mere coincidence.

Patty G.
Naples, Florida

Whatever It Takes
December 2008

T he cute blond on the barstool reached out her hands for me. "Hey, Sweetie, did you find the ladies' room?" I nodded my head. As a matter of fact I had, but this young lady had me confused with someone else.

As a recovering alcoholic of a year and a half, I inwardly smiled at inebriated ladies. Because I am a spoken word poet, I still sometimes frequent nightclubs and bars—strictly sober this time. "Oh, I'm sorry," she said, obviously embarrassed. "You are not who I thought you were. I'm afraid I've had a bit too much to drink."

"No problem," I answered pleasantly. "I certainly understand. That has happened to me."

The bartender refilled my glass with club soda and a lime. Although I had never chatted with him about my sobriety, he knew me well enough to keep those club sodas coming.

When I got sober, I was concerned that I would have to give up my stage appearances and my social life. Through the power of the Twelve Steps, I have learned how to avoid alcohol and continue the art I love. I had begun drinking because of my constant contact with nightclubs. Just a glass of wine here and there. Then more.

Four years later, I was a full-fledged alcoholic waking up with the shakes, downing 18 ounces of straight Scotch every night, and driving to work with a hangover every morning. That was just the weekdays.

The weekends were far worse. Every Sunday I stayed in bed nursing a hangover.

A good party was when I vomited on the way home so I could sleep without the dizzy bed syndrome. My performances were characterized by slurring and giggling. I could no longer walk across a stage or daintily step over microphone cords.

What had started out to be fun had become a nightmare. The last year I drank, I lost part of my liver function. Through AA, I learned how to deal with life on its own terms and enjoy myself in the environment I still loved. The alcohol was not a threat to me. I knew what horror hid inside the bottle.

The young lady was now asking, "Don't you drink?"

"Not any more," I said, and tried to change the subject. I work hard to not make an issue out of my sobriety when I am out. I was at a poetry open mike with people who chose to drink—not at a meeting!

She wouldn't let it drop. "You used to drink?" she persisted.

"Yes," I said. "I learned I couldn't handle it. Have you heard this poet before?" I asked.

"When did you know you had to stop?" She was looking at me quite earnestly now, ignoring the poet on the stage. She really wanted to know. Suddenly I recognized that look she was giving me. She was asking for help.

Gently, I took her by the arm and led her to a quiet spot in the club. In a lowered voice, I told her some of my story. I asked her some of the questions from the AA World Services website. I ended by saying, "If you are asking yourself that question, the time to stop is probably now. Later, you may not be able to."

I told her to get in touch with AA and prayed with her to the clink of glasses and the beat of the music. That night on stage, I chose to do my "drunk poem," where I tell my story in spoken word verse. She watched me raptly. As I left the club, she smiled and waved. Her husband thanked me.

I learned that night that there is no perfect time to share the message. I must be available whenever and wherever my Higher Power needs me. I have wondered about that woman many times. Wherever she is, I hope she is doing well. I listen carefully to people out in public now. My reluctance to avoid preaching almost kept me from sharing a message with someone who was asking for help.

Lori T.
Grand Prairie, Texas

Eyeliner, Anyone?
July 2004

During my first nine years of sobriety, I had learned that the grouches I liked to display didn't get me what I wanted or needed, and I did not give in to this old behavior frequently. But the brainstorm? I valued my brainstorms and believed that that part of the Big Book surely wasn't meant for me. How much I still had to learn.

In my ninth year of sobriety, I was fired as part of a staff reduction at work because of the sagging economy in our area. I was devastated. Anger always comes first with me, masking the feelings of rejection, abandonment, self-pity, and last but never least—pride.

The people in AA were compassionate and supportive. I was given many suggestions, some based on experience, some on other people's brainstorms. I followed through on the more practical suggestions, applying for unemployment, submitting applications to places that could use my skills, opening my mind to a new career path and talking it over with my Higher Power to ask for his help.

But after I had taken all of the actions, I found it hard to sit and wait. I always had been an action-oriented person and took pride in tackling problems head-on. "Don't just sit there, do something" was my war cry. Unfortunately, I mistook frantic activity—based on brainstorms—for well-thought-out action. I thought my brainstorms were God-inspired solutions.

Webster's dictionary says a brainstorm is "a violent transient mental derangement," in other words, "a harebrained idea." I had to do something and when I heard about someone else's brainstorm, I took it for my own. I invested my retirement funds in a party-plan cosmetics dealership. When I filled out a questionnaire to see if I was fit for this line of work, I failed it miserably. But the people at headquarters must have been on break when my form came in, because they quickly cashed my check, sent me 20 boxes of cosmetics and wished me great luck.

After I'd sold cosmetics to my reluctant friends and family, my little business died. I just did not have what it took to be successful in such an endeavor. The questionnaire knew it; now I knew it.

Looking back, I see I was like a person sitting in a train depot, clutching a ticket, waiting for her scheduled train. But waiting is difficult, so I jumped on the first train that started to move, not knowing what city it was going to or even if it was going in the right direction.

When I first became unemployed, I took the necessary actions and turned the outcome over to the Higher Power. I should have waited for God to do his work. Instead, I went with the first brainstorm that came along. In God's time, I was hired back by my former employer in a different position, which I liked far better than my old one.

The lessons learned were expensive in terms of time, money and serenity, but I did learn to wait for the right train. By the way, does anyone want to buy some eyeliner?

N.H
Sterling, Illinois

Escape Artist
December 2010

I am in college at age 53, studying graphic design—something I never thought of doing in my entire life, but something that brings me joy and friendship. My sponsor works as a student liaison and insisted that I try taking one class. Here I am, almost 54, and finally ready to have a college degree in a field that makes me wonder why people pay you to have this much fun.

At one point I was ready to quit. I wasn't good enough, wasn't as talented ... blah, blah, blah. One of the professors saw me crying and asked what was up. It turned out she knew exactly what to say. "Well, all that might be true or it might not," She said. "Maybe you should quit. But before you do, ask yourself: What's worse, quitting or failing?"

For the first time in my life, I realized that I've always quit (even sobriety) because I am terrified of success and terrified of failure. If I succeed, I might have to do something with my God-given talent. If I fail, I have to face it. Lucky for me, I have the disease of alcoholism. I came home and created from my heart the words and images in a photo illustration of how I felt.

You know what happened? I didn't quit. And I got the award in that class for that semester. I am so blessed to have stayed sober long enough for the miracles to begin. I am so grateful for the students and faculty who pulled me through. I am grateful to God for a second chance and my sponsor for suggesting changes with love. Recently I faced depression again. I know that if I can face it and act my way into good thinking, I may just find more rainbows in my life.

Cindy M.
Hollywood, Florida

Pandora's Bottle
August 1951

I was the girl who loved her work—loved it, lived in it, drowned in it, did it too many hours a day and then took it home to run around in my head at night. Dull jobs I couldn't bear—I interviewed fascinating people about this-and-that, I had a way with printers, I could write headlines with a sting in the tail and a double pun in the middle.

I was a ball of fire on every job I ever had—while I lasted. I was a fiend for overtime; bosses loved me. Not one of them understood why I took off, under my own power, before many months. They offered me raises and wanted me back. None of them ever saw inside my head at night, where type and paste-pots and double-pun headlines went round and round, faster and faster. None of them ever saw the demons who sat on my shoulder and screamed at me until I could no longer run away from them into work, and drowned them in a bottle.

Then, for awhile, I would be so tired I couldn't run, the demons would hide in their cave and go to sleep for a little, and while they slept I wouldn't need the bottle.

Until the next time.

There was, finally, what had to be the last next time—the time when the demons came out of the bottle bigger and more terrifying than they went into it, and I knew they couldn't be drowned and it was no good running any longer.

I was fresh out of a job when I came to AA, and I was fresh out of money. I was too tired to run. Eating, by some means or other, looked important. I took a straight look at my trade—the strenuous, I'm-a-smart-girl trade which had been helping to drive me to drink.

What was a job, really? Not something to take home at night. Not something to make a life from. Not something to build the ego on.

Not something to run away into, until there was nothing left of me to run. Just a way to eat and pay the rent and a couple of bills, that was all a job was.

But I was lucky. The work I knew entailed a lot of unexciting, non-ego-building skills. A small-time editor has to type, and read proof, and talk to people. Maybe if I did just one of them, not the whole batch and a few dozen other things besides, a little of me would be left over to learn to live with myself. Maybe if I didn't run so hard, there wouldn't be so much to run from.

Not drinking seemed to me then, as it still does, even more important than eating. I wanted to go to lots of meetings, and to think about them. I needed to work, but I knew that I never again wanted to tackle a job that took all of me. I said a quick little what-do-I-do prayer in a telephone booth, and called the plush employment agency which had sent me out with fanfare on the last of the bright-girl jobs. Any kind of work I could do please, I said, as long as it was temporary. They were startled, having dealt with me when nothing they offered was spectacular enough for me; but they were cooperative.

Typing and reading proof and talking to people, not all on the same job, but one at a time—has proved a good road back for this alcoholic. Nothing much stands or falls by a temporary job, they come fairly easy, there's no ego involved and no hurt when they end, and the dullest work in the world is the best way to practice living a day at a time. I, who never could stand routine, typed addresses for four months for a credit house. I, who was above ringing doorbells, rang them, doing market research, taking census. I, who could handle only sparkling copy, read proof on ream after whereas-studded monotonous ream of legal notices. You don't buy mink coats that way, but you pay the rent, and five dollars here and a couple of dollars there, you whittle away at the bills.

For me it has been a good way to approach the Fifth Step, a good way to find out what I'm really like. All the years before, I'd been busy running. At first I was too confused to do much after work except go to meetings, and I was terrified of myself and of responsibility. The hours spent at an unimportant repetitive task were good for me. What I'd learned at meetings had time, through the undemanding days, to sink in. I found I liked myself better, and was happier with other people, now that I wasn't in competition with them trying to be smarty-pants. I built up confidence in myself as I learned to do a dull job well and to be content in doing it. Evenings, with energy left over from work for the first time in my life, I began to try some of the things I'd always wanted to do and been ashamed to admit I didn't know. I, who had never been able to sew a straight seam, took a course in dressmaking. I who always thought I couldn't use my hands, learned to knit, and loved it.

Sometimes there was a day or two, or a week, between jobs. It didn't panic me and it didn't hurt my new-found dignity. I had no face to lose, now that I wasn't trying to maintain face. Each uncharted day I did everything I could to find the next job, and then if it didn't rear its head, I took the free time as a delightful gift and used it accordingly. I made Twelfth Step telephone calls. I went to museums. I drank endless, leisurely coffee with my sponsor. I walked in the sunshine and window-shopped.

If the demons came out of their caves, as they still did occasionally, I had time to learn new, sober ways of dealing with them. They didn't scream as loudly in my ear as they once did. I began to learn to run away from them into reading, or to talk, fast and endlessly, until they were as tired as I was. I began to look them in the eye and to see where they came from, and, as I looked, to watch them take to their terrible black wings and fly away for keeps, one by one.

Slowly, in the hours left after the jobs which were neither ego-building nor exhausting, and in the days between jobs, I found that I was learning to live a life with a lot of new facets. I was turning into a contented woman with a lot of quiet, pleasant interests, and not a hardbitten gal with a career that didn't quite come off. I was learning to be a whole person, integrated, all in one piece, and not just a tangle of screaming neuroses running away from each other.

After a while the temporary jobs sort of ran together. The one I have now looks like lasting. It uses a few of the old skills, but it isn't smarty-pants. The boss likes me because I'm easy to get along with, which AA taught me to be, not because I put in overtime, which I don't.

I can still make double puns if I must, but only by daylight. They don't run around in my head at night; I shut them away under the typewriter cover and leave them at the office. I'm a gal who likes her work reasonably well; but what's a job, really? Just a way to eat, and pay the rent and whittle away at the bills.

I'll never have the price of a mink coat, and it doesn't matter. I'd rather have this new self.

M. C.
Hollywood, California

CHAPTER NINE

Lifelong Friends

———— * ————

Sober women finding new, often unexpected, friendships

Our literature talks about the alcoholic being "tortured by loneliness." For many, alcoholism isolated us from others and made true friendship difficult, when not impossible. In AA, that changes as the stories in the following chapter surely attest.

"I was never one for female relationships," writes Cheryl B. in the story "Hanging With the Girls." "I was much more comfortable with men." Now she says AA women "helped save my life" and have become her dear friends.

In "Florida or Bust," Susan B. and her best friend live parallel self-destructive lives and eventually get sober together. Read here how their friendship endures.

L.B. writes in "One Woman's Journey" about the help other women in the program gave her. She found herself experiencing a "new feeling of sisterhood, a feeling that I'd never experienced."

In her story "In Good Company," Holly H. writes about fulfilling a dream to go whitewater rafting, but having to walk through the fear by herself. When she arrives at the river, she's met by a big surprise and ends up having the day of her life with a host of new friends.

Hanging With the Girls
March 2012

I was never one for female relationships. I had had a couple of friends here and there through the years, but I was much more comfortable with the men. I found them easier to get along with whether they were romantic relationships or not. Woman seemed to be backstabbers and catty gossips. I had no use for them.

I was almost paralyzed by the idea of trying to socialize without my best friend alcohol and now, new to AA, I was being told to go to talk with these women. What would we talk about? I never felt very "girly girly" and I was sure they wouldn't like me.

As I tried to live this new way of life, it didn't take long for me to figure out that would be a big piece to my sobriety. The pull of my disease was killing me and I realized I was going to need these women if I were going to stay here. Handling it alone was not going to work for me. And entirely relying on my sponsor would be unreasonable and I would be cheating myself of friendships, as she kindly explained.

And so I began—slowly and grudgingly—getting to know some women in the beginners' meeting I was attending. That is where I met the women who would become my dear friends throughout my entire sobriety thus far. We may be in different stages and places in our lives today, but we are all still sober and that is the miracle of this program!

I began reaching out to them with phone calls. As a single mother, I needed the other sober moms to help me get through life's everyday challenges. Being new in the program, every little thing felt monumental to me. By sharing my feelings and thoughts, they would help carry the weight and I could make it through without picking up a drink one day at a time.

A lot of times by the end of the phone call, we would have had at least one laugh, which helped ease the stress I was feeling and put things back into perspective. I would also listen to them and what they had going on, which aided me in forgetting about myself for a millisecond. The bottom line was that I would always feel better when I got off the phone.

My relationships with them continued to build and strengthen through fellowship at restaurants, retreats and driving to meetings together. We learned how to dance sober together. At one point, some of us were even on a women's sober softball team.

We dealt with exes, mothers, fathers and family members and raised our children together, all the while staying sober. AA taught us that to have a friend, you need to be a friend. I had no clue how to do this. My past had taught me that if someone made me mad or did something I didn't like, to cross them off my list. This is the real reason I had no friends when I came into the rooms. Through these AA friendships, I have learned and am still learning how to handle "differences" as they arise, instead of ending the relationship.

I try to live and let live and apply these tools to all of my relationships, in and out of the program. The key word being "try"—this stuff does not come easy to me at all. It is a miracle I have been able to sustain these friendships, but that is a testimony to Alcoholics Anonymous and working the Steps.

Sometimes in life, there are things that I can only talk to another alcoholic about. I still need their love and support, especially when my alcoholism rears its ugly head and tries to get the best of me by telling me I'm good now, I don't need to go to those meetings anymore. I am accountable to my friends and I can only hope I have been there for them as much as they have been for me.

Thank God for these women. The women I wanted nothing to do with. The women who have helped save my life.

Cheryl B.
North Riverside, Illinois

Florida or Bust
January 2017

We were three sober women, traveling 1100 miles from Dayton, Ohio to Pine Island, Florida to visit a mutual AA friend. And even though we had never before spent that much time together, we were excited and had great expectations, anticipating the warm air and white sand. We left at 3:30 in the morning. We wanted to drive for nine hours and stop at a hotel at the halfway point of our journey so we could soak up some southern rays by a pool.

We left with a prayer for our safe journey. But no more than 20 miles outside Dayton, red flashing lights stopped us. The running lights on our trailer—which held three kayaks, one bike and all our camping gear— were not working correctly. The police officer warned us to get the lights checked, pronto. So, off we headed to a place where we could get new wiring to replace the bad.

As we pulled away from the berm where we had been pulled over, our car hit a torn tire tread lying by the road that nearly caused us to lose control. We continued on to find a store, and tried and tried to get the wiring connectors to work as the packaging suggested. We were getting nowhere. Then, in a last-ditch attempt, we wired them all together and voila!, we had running lights again.

Of course, while lying on the cold ground to replace the bad wiring we noticed that something underneath the car had been ripped loose by the tire tread we had hit. Not even 60 miles and just three hours away from our starting point, we had already been challenged on our journey. But we hoped we had put the worst of our troubles behind us and forged ahead, laughing and, not being a glum lot, anticipating good times to come. Whatever had been torn loose by the tire would be taken care of by a mechanic when we arrived at our final destination.

The next four hours went pretty smoothly and we shared a lot about ourselves and experiences in and out of AA. Then a warning ding began to sound off from the car's computer, indicating some sort of problem. Was it caused by the piece we'd seen hanging under the car? We didn't know, so we agreed to add it to the list of things that would be checked out by the mechanic in Florida.

By the time we arrived at our halfway point, it was too late to enjoy the pool. We entered the supposedly four-star motel where we had room reservations. But what we found was a long way from four stars. So, off to another motel we went. Well, that was not better than the first. Off we went to a third motel. We were so exhausted that none of us were willing to say it was too small, and by morning we were willing to say that the mattresses were pretty nice.

Our next destination was a beautiful campground in Ft. De Soto, Florida. Oh, it was beautiful alright. But Florida was not the 70 degrees we had anticipated when we packed for the trip. No, it was about 45 degrees and raining. Exhausted and nearly spent, we decided to wait out the rain and get something to eat before setting up our campsite. Feeling for our girl, the owner of the trailer and toys, who was feeling "in the hole," we went to the restaurant she suggested and then to a hardware store to buy a new tarp, because the one covering her trailer had been whipped to pieces.

Raincoats were in order, but the store was sold out. We bought Visqueen to make ourselves temporary covers while we set up our site in the steady rain. We soon learned that leaving the doors to the car open was a bad idea. A pack of raccoons in the park had turned our car into a munching ground of treats. The tent we were setting up had a broken pole and we all struggled as we tried to keep a tarp over the screened ceiling of the tent so we could be dry while we slept. Patience was wearing thin for all of us.

Winds whipped through the campground the following day. But we were still in fair spirits, waiting on the good weather we had so anxiously anticipated. We made the best of a bad situation and checked out the local history of Ft. De Soto and walked the beaches along the

Gulf of Mexico while the strong wind blew sand and cold waves at us.

Finally, the sun broke through on the fourth day and we lay on the beach, digging our bare feet into the sand. One of us curled in a blanket. We were having the moments of peace and serenity we had wanted to find in Florida and were working our individual programs and thanking our Higher Power as we understood him or her for the bit of sun, regardless of the sand buzzards (seagulls) stealing our snacks.

As of that moment, none of the toys had been used. Waves were too high for kayaking or fishing, and by the next day it was time to leave for our final destination to visit our spiritual guru, who helped us each recognize the challenges we had overcome.

Finally, we made it. On Pine Island, the sun began to shine brighter, the temperature rose, and, $400 later, the car was repaired. We all rode bikes. The kayaks entered water. We ate fish we didn't catch, attended an AA meeting, played cards, drank smoothies and ate fruit. We laughed and smiled.

Reading this, you might be wondering what our story has to do with sobriety. Well, we didn't drink. We didn't tear the arms off each other as we struggled to set up the tent in the rain. We didn't scratch eyes out fighting for what each thought we should do next.

Each of us had been tried and tested in one way or the other during our trek. The principles of AA—honesty, hope, faith, courage, integrity, willingness, humility, understanding, discipline, perseverance, spirituality and responsibility—each had played their part. And we headed home—1100 miles away, through sub-zero weather and snow—with memorable and happy experiences of our journey

Susan B.
Dayton, Ohio

Look Out for Two Old Ladies
May 2013

My favorite friend and I met way back on a bright fall day in the mid-70s. We were fresh teenagers wearing peasant outfits while working at the local steakhouse. I don't know who thought of the idea first, but we found that work was extremely fun with tumblers full of rum and coke hidden in our hostess stand. We bonded over those and many, many other alcoholic moments. It was fun—and disastrous.

Over the years, my friend Christine and I appeared to live parallel self-destructive lives. We moved to Arizona and both found dead-end relationships. I eventually came back to my hometown in 1985. I had heard of AA through my mother's attempt to get sober. I thought if she could do it, then maybe I could too.

At 27 years old, I found myself living at home. I was so delusional I thought I had to hide my liquor from family members, but nobody ever seemed interested in finding it, let alone taking it away from me. After I got sober I came to find out many alcoholics hide their liquor— even when there is no one around to find or touch it. It took many attempts, a lot of one-on-one sessions with a sober therapist, and getting down on my knees a few times, before sobriety finally saved me in October 1985.

A few years later, my best friend also eventually returned to our hometown with her baby daughter. We ran into each other after losing contact for those few years. I was able to tell her of my sobriety. She congratulated me and gave me a big hug. Shortly thereafter I got a call from her. She was interested in checking out AA. It stuck for her right away, and she found her sobriety in February of 1988. Since that time we have both enjoyed continuous sobriety.

The best part of having my best friend sober with me is that we both love to travel, laugh, shop and get pampered—things better off done with a great friend, instead of a husband who doesn't quite understand the finer feelings of enjoying a great cup of coffee while soaking your feet in a pedicure tub and yakking away with your buddy.

Through following directions from our sponsors and other strong women in the program, Christine was able to raise a wonderful daughter. Rachel grew up in AA meetings; first in a carrier, then a stroller and finally with crayons and coloring books in tow. My support system saw me through an associate's degree, a bachelor of arts and finally a master's degree. Through diligence and love, both of us have sober lives filled with many of the Promises. It has afforded us jobs we like and the ability to travel. We don't go on luxury cruises or five-star tours, but we do find inexpensive ways to have fun. She lives on the West Coast and I live on the East Coast. About once or twice a year we plan an excursion to a different city for shopping, walking and touring. We've met in Portland for great food, Santa Fe for beautiful weather, Tucson and Sedona for sunshine and shopping, Chicago for stunning architecture and Las Vegas for a show of her favorite comedian. Anytime you travel with Christine she'll pull out her comedy CDs and get the laughter started quickly.

I'm a hiker, skier, dog-and-cat kind of person; Christine is more of the art-festivals-in-the-city type of woman. But she is definitely more adventurous than I am. She'll find coupons for a luxury stay in Thailand and go off on an adventure of her own. A few years ago, she finally convinced me that getting a passport wasn't a challenging ordeal. She told me fear was only "false evidence appearing real" and that I should go for it. I did. Little did I know I would soon find myself eating bologna sandwiches at 3 A.M. (San Francisco time), as we flew to Sydney, Australia. If you want to have a great time in sobriety, find a kangaroo to feed! It's fantastic. Try to get your best friend to stand next to a huge peacock and take her picture. Or even better, if you find yourself in Arizona, try to get her to go stand by a wild brahma bull. Tell her it will make a great holiday photo.

Christine and I have known each other for 35 years; combined we have over 50 years of sobriety. Things that appear to keep us young are cheap trips, thrift shops, much laughter and a thorough enjoyment and appreciation for our sobriety. We both still go to meetings, have sponsors and work strong programs. We both also have very busy careers and lives with our families.

It's one of the most calming and enjoyable parts of my life to know I have someone to call who always has my back and who can always make me laugh. Find a friend, enjoy sobriety and find a museum, walking path or park bench. Enjoy a great cup of coffee, some one-to-one fellowship and wonderful laughter. And if you find yourself in Belize this holiday season, look out for two old ladies—one will be trying to convince the other that baboons and howler monkeys at the sanctuary will make a great picture—if she would just move in a little closer!

Helen H.
Pittsburgh, Pennsylvania

One Woman's Journey
June 1979

This is not intended as a treatise on sex. Nor do I claim that women are special in their recovery through AA or have a tougher time of it than men. My purpose here is to share my experience, strength and hope as a single woman who is a recovering alcoholic.

When I first entered an AA meeting room in 1971, in a middle-sized southeastern city, there was one other woman who attended meetings there regularly. She and I had a great many things in common, including a lack of acceptance and a refusal to admit powerlessness.

I did not continue to attend meetings, nor did I read any of the literature. Even though my new friend and I knew a third woman who had died a painful alcoholic death, neither of us seemed to get the message that day, and we both went out and drank some more.

In the ensuing years, I lost jobs and friends, and my health became impaired. When I came again to an AA meeting room, I was there for a meeting. I came; I came to; I surrendered; I came to believe.

My health began to improve. By then, there were many more women in the program, and they talked me through the first few difficult 24 hours. I began to take a renewed interest—long-dormant—in my appearance, and when the fog lifted a bit, I was looking better than I had in years. I had a little makeup on, my clothes were matching, my hair was clean and I was beginning to feel human again. Even more amazingly, I was beginning to feel like a female human being again!

An old-timer in our meeting told me that he had gotten sober through "brute strength and awkwardness." I remembered that saying daily, because it so aptly described, not only my avoidance of the first drink, but also my handling of new situations.

My emotions were returning, and this time they were undiluted by booze. I experienced my first sober trip to the dentist, then my first sober cold, then my first sober pass. I handled them all awkwardly, particularly the pass.

Dealing with sudden attention from men didn't get easier right away. I felt like a schoolgirl. I was awkward and confused, and I faced my first sober dilemma: Should I continue to work on my appearance and expect to be noticed by men, or should I put a bag over my head and get on with my program? Did one endeavor necessarily preclude the other?

I struggled with almost every aspect of my life during those early few 24 hours. Simple mechanical tasks were baffling, and the more complex ones were more so. Struggling with this new dilemma raised old fears, doubts, problems of self-esteem.

At that point, I began to approach the problem in ways that I'd never before considered. I used some of the tools of the program, though they were still new and a bit strange to me. I talked to AA friends, to many women both older and younger than I. I briefly took the podium at an open participation meeting and spoke in general terms about the dilemma I was experiencing. My sponsor, who wasn't giving advice, told me of some people's opinion that newcomers might do well to avoid dilemmas in general and emotional involvements in particular for an unspecified time.

When I'd been in the program six weeks, a married man paid some attention to me after a meeting, and I was instantly in love—or, more accurately, was instantly obsessed. I began to think of this man constantly. I dreamed of him. I built fantasy worlds in which we were running away together. I was uncomfortable in the same meeting with him and embarrassed around his wife, and all this from a few casual, friendly remarks.

The obsession passed, but the lesson I learned endured. I could see that I was immensely vulnerable as a new non-drinking alcoholic. During my drinking years, I had used alcohol to help me deal with social situations, and toward the end, I had cut myself off from all interaction. I did not realize how lonely I had become until the obsession helped me to see the social effects of my drinking.

So this was why the old-timers had suggested that I avoid emotional involvements. In my confusion, I simply didn't know how to handle situations with a very clear head. I was still an emotional infant with an adult appearance.

After the first 90 days, I stuck close to the program and attended many meetings. I let men know how long I had in the program and explained that I still felt too new (or "not sober enough") to go on dates.

And I prayed, awkwardly at first. I asked for forgiveness for the confusion I was having. Then I prayed that I might have the extra strength I needed and some idea of His will for my life. I got it down to one 24-hour period at a time.

My dilemma became a good bit easier to deal with and I became less awkward when I was able to be honest about what I wanted, what my priorities were. When I knew who I was and what I wanted, the confusion subsided greatly. I am an alcoholic. I want to be sober.

My feelings about men may have been warped, but so were my feelings about other women. My experience in regard to other women also began to change after I came to the program.

A speaker at one birthday meeting said something that made me mildly uncomfortable. She said that at the time of her beginning in AA, she did not like other women and did not trust them. She had been working in a man's world, and she found she identified more with business concerns than with what she saw as the frivolous activities of housewives.

When I gave some honest thought to that speech, I had to admit that I felt that way too. I had few close women friends, and I actually considered myself above "woman's work." Suddenly, admitting my own prejudices made me alone responsible for them.

And I began to discover how wrong I had been. The other AA women may not have been much different from women in general, but I was discovering that we had more things in common than I'd imagined. I experienced a new feeling of sisterhood, a feeling that I'd never experienced in the wake of the women's movement.

More and more, I was turning to other women in the program to share problems, experiences and concerns. I added a regular women's meeting to my schedule, and my growing telephone list is made up almost entirely of women.

I was no longer suspicious of the intentions of men, nor was I particularly trying to avoid speaking to them. But I was finding that, in my case, my recovery was aided best by calling other women when I had a problem.

And strangely enough for me, I was enjoying the company of other AA women. Before coming into the program, I tended to consider an evening meal with a woman friend as but a substitute for a date with a man. Now, I am becoming contented with the company of women friends and have turned down dates in order to have dinner or see a movie with a group of other women.

I am never finished, but today I am on the journey I began as a child. If my sharing helps others, then I am better for that. Finally, I am understanding what this saying means: It is not the end that matters; it is the journey that matters in the end.

L. B.
Atlanta, Georgia

In Good Company
June 2016

I t was Memorial Day weekend, 1991. I was 38 years old at the time, two years sober, and quite happy about it all. The initial fog had started to lift, and it seemed like God had given me the world wrapped in a red bow and said, "Go. Enjoy. Just don't drink."

One thing I had always wanted to do was whitewater rafting, even though I knew not one thing about it. But that's what a phone is for, right? I picked out a rafting place at random from the phone book and called for information. It sounded easy enough. I would dress comfortably, show up at the river and be put in a group of other rafters.

But I ran into a problem. Despite my carpe diem sweatshirt and easy smile, I could not find one solitary soul, in the program or out of it, to go with me on my Memorial Day rafting adventure. So the trip would be my first adventure alone and sober. I was scared. But sobriety is all about new experiences, isn't it? So I decided to go anyway, with only my Higher Power to accompany me.

In my short time in AA, I had been given many examples of how a Higher Power worked in my life. And I listened when people in the program said, "Nothing, absolutely nothing, in God's world happens by mistake."

So with joy in my heart, gas in my car and an empty passenger seat at my side, I set off for Ohiopyle, a trip of about two hours, to do what I had dreamed of doing for 20 years. I turned to the empty seat and said, "This is great." The seat said nothing.

Showing up at Ohiopyle, I pulled into the large unpaved parking lot surrounded on all sides by various kiosk-type huts selling rafting trips. While looking for a spot to park, I noticed several cars with bumper stickers that said, "Higher Powered," "One Day At A Time" and "Friend Of Bill." What were the chances?

So I set out to find the hut with the most alcoholic-looking people I could find. At that point in my recovery I figured I could probably tell by looking. I settled on a hut and was assigned to a rafting group. Were any of these the AA bumper sticker people?

Our guide from the hut outfitted us with helmets and lifejackets and gave us our six-person raft. We were assigned seats on the raft, with me sitting in the front-right spot. Instructions were given, rafting skills explained, and once we were in our raft and practicing in the river, lots of inadvertent paddling in circles and raucous laughter followed. Imagine that, I thought. I can actually have fun with "earth people" too. Since most of my time until that point in recovery had been spent with people from the program, this was a new experience in more ways than one.

Off we went to begin our trek down the river.

The first set of rapids approached. When we got to it, one person fell out of the raft. It was not me. We regrouped. The second set of rapids approached, and one person dropped their oar in the water. It was not me. Again, we regrouped. The third set of rapids approached, and we got stuck on the rock. And, yes, it was me who got stuck. But we regrouped.

By the time we approached the fourth set of rapids, we were laughing together like the seasoned rafting veterans we felt ourselves to be. I had long since given up my efforts to figure out who among our rafting crew, if any, was a drunk like me—although my money would have been on Mr. Back Left.

The fourth set of rapids was challenging. It had lots of obstacles, lots of whitewater and lots of big rocks. But none of us fell out. No one lost an oar. We steered clear through. But we went over backwards. Laughing. And Miss Middle Left said, "Well, you know what they say, 'It's progress, not perfection.'"

Time stopped. Could it be? Was she the drunk I had been seeking? And if so, how would I go about letting her know I was one too? I couldn't just ask, "Are you a drunk like me?" What if she wasn't? And then there was the anonymity thing. I thought about dropping a hint, like saying, "One paddle at a time." Better to just be silent and wait till lunch, I decided, at which point I cornered Miss Middle Left where I could not be overheard.

"Hey, I liked what you said back there, that 'progress, not perfection' thing." I said. "Where did you ever get that from?" I thought I was being pretty smooth. "Well," she answered, "I just heard it around." Wow, I thought, earth people used terms like that too. But then, after a short pause, she added, "... around the rooms."

I was stunned and started excitely talking. "Oh my gosh," I said, "I'm also in the program and I saw all those bumper stickers in the parking lot. I thought there might be a drunk out here somewhere. But I never would have guessed that you ..." Babbling at its finest. She stopped me and said, "Yes, I am in the program. As a matter of fact, everyone in our raft is in the program. Except for that newlywed couple over there, all 60 of us in this group are in the program."

My mouth fell open and she excitedly walked back toward the group yelling, "Hey everyone! Holly here is a friend of Bill's too!" And in true AA fashion, I was welcomed with open arms into the group of drunks who had traveled up that day from Maryland. I spent the rest of the trip with my new friends, laughing and paddling and enjoying the special fellowship that is found in AA. At the end of the trip down the river they invited me back to their campsite, where we shared a wonderful dinner outdoors and an AA meeting around the campfire.

Just like they say in the Big Book, I was right where I needed to be. What were the chances of me going on a rafting trip by myself and ending up on that day, at that particular time, at that kiosk, so that I got to raft with that group?

There was no doubt in my mind that day that my Higher Power was looking after me. It was almost as if there were writing in the sky, saying something like, "Don't worry Holly, I've got it under control."

Holly H.
Altoona, Pennsylvania

The Laugh-Out-Loud List
May 2011

I was just over a year sober, and Nicole and I were lying on the floor of my living room. The first year of my sobriety was propelled by me getting really involved, doing the Steps and going to a lot of meetings. I was good. I was living sobriety and breathing in a new way.

So we lay there on the floor with paper and pen, because I had just gotten the wild idea that we should make this list. "Let's call it the Laugh-Out-Loud List," I told her. "We'll make a list of all of the things that make us laugh out loud when we think about them. This way, if we're ever in a depressing place, in a bind, stuck in indecision, we can have this on the refrigerator, take a look at it and break out laughing."

What a Higher Power-inspired idea. As we made our lists, we were cracking up and busting a gut, just by remembering things that were funny. As the weeks and months went on, we added to our lists. We referenced our lists. On the phone with each other, after sharing a particularly funny incident, one of us would demand that it go on the list.

It was on a piece of notebook paper, and through adding to it over time the list became wrinkled and faded. But the idea prospered. I made a new one. I made another one. I made one for work too, and at the end of the work year, I typed it up for my department and we had a get-together where we went over it and just kept cracking up.

I can't relay any blinding light experiences that came from this, but this "spiritual experience of the educational variety" has made it a readily available option for me to stop in a bad moment, think of something hilarious and change my thought. My understanding is that this is what being truly sober is about: changing my thinking through divine inspiration.

Ginny M.
Lehigh Acres, Florida

CHAPTER TEN

Women's Meetings

————— ✳ —————

Women find fellowship and recovery together

AA *meetings specifically for women have long been present in the Fellowship. For many women alcoholics, women's meetings have served as a helpful gateway to the general Fellowship as well as an important part of their sobriety long-term. Here are personal stories about women's meetings from around the globe.*

Jody Y. thought women were "Pollyannas going on and on" until her sponsor encourages her to get a different perspective by attending a women's meeting. She becomes a regular.

In her story "Oreos and a T-Shirt," Granny M. tells the story of a member of her online womens group who turns to the group to come to terms with the day she drove drunk, killing her husband and children.

A lesbian AA from Boston, in "Let Others Win the Ribbons," moves back to her small hometown in Arkansas, where she finds needed support from her Friday night women's meeting.

In "Winnipeg Women Celebrate the Big Five-O," a women's group in Canada celebrates its 50th anniversary and reveals the reasons for its longevity through the social twists and turns of the past five decades.

In "Meeting at Shivaji Market," Deborah D. travels to India—where female alcoholics can feel "immense shame" and struggle to find sobriety—and helps start an AA meeting there for women.

Don't Sugarcoat It
February 2010

Oh, the power, the joy, the awesomeness of 45 women in one room saying the Lord's Prayer at the end of what turned out to be a gratitude meeting. This is why I am still on this journey with these women. This is why I love service work. This is why my passion is to help women get sober and get their power back. Meetings like these give meaning to the pain, heartbreak, loss and sorrow of the childhood I survived, the recovery I have been able to achieve. This is the reason to share my experience, strength and hope with all women struggling with this disease. I tell them they must never give up hope or quit quitting. There are women all over the world doing just what you and I are doing each day: living—one day at a time—sober, powerful, meaningful lives without alcohol.

Life continues to happen even in sobriety. The difference is that we no longer feel we have to tough life out alone. We have the tools of the program to show us how to ask for help, receive the unconditional love and support of other women and get through whatever it is sober.

Did I buy all that early on, before joining a women's group? Heck no! I thought they were all a bunch of Pollyannas going on and on. No way could I ever be grateful for being alcoholic. Join a women's meeting? "I won't do meetings of any kind with a bunch of women who gossip, cut me down and are prettier or smarter than me," I said. But my sponsor insisted and I eventually stayed sober.

So when I moved to a different city with no women's meeting, five other women and I started one, and it has grown tremendously over the past 12 years. Some of us are taking meetings to the local jail. We started getting referrals from the courts, treatment centers and counselors. We started a Big Book study on Saturdays, and we grew.

No matter what, we are there to sponsor new women and help them. We show them it is possible to stop giving all their power to alcohol. We love them until they can love themselves. And slowly, they begin to trust us—even if we are women. That kind of unconditional love was what none of us had until we got here. With the help, they begin to envision a future with peace, freedom, joy and serenity. They begin helping other newcomers like themselves. And so it goes: that wonderful act of paying it forward.

One of my sponsees likes to tell new women at First Step meetings, "Prepare to be uncomfortable. You will be, and you will live through it. There are still days I am in pain, sad, frustrated, anxious or uncomfortable. But today, I talk to my sponsor or another recovering woman about it, and I get better. I do not have to pick up."

I love that she doesn't sugarcoat it. Because the truth is that this is the hardest thing most of us have ever done. Not only do we learn to live without alcohol, we learn a whole new way of life that gives us our power back as women.

There is a lot of wreckage from our past that we have to clean up. Some of it is pretty tough. Some may not get their husbands, jobs or even their children back. That is the reality we may have to deal with. But if we continue to drink, we will lose all of it anyway for sure. Tough stuff. But if we are finally sick and tired enough, if we have finally become willing to follow suggestions, then just maybe we have a chance. And what a gift that willingness is.

It is truly the grace of our Higher Power that gets us and keeps us sober—that and a little help from friends. If my experience, strength and hope can help just one woman get sober and get her power back, then it is always worth showing up at a meeting and sharing. This is my passion and what keeps me coming back.

Jody Y.
South Lyon, Michigan

Winnipeg Women Celebrate the Big Five-O
August 2003

In February 2003, the Winnipeg Women's Group in Winnipeg, Manitoba, celebrated its 50th anniversary, making it, they've been told, the oldest women's group in Alcoholics Anonymous to function continuously for that length of time. —The Editors

AA was established in Winnipeg on November 26, 1944. By 1953, there were four groups, with only a few women members in each. When one of these women, Isobel G., mentioned to her psychiatrist that she would like to be in a women's group, he put her in touch with Therese C. from the Assiniboine Group, and they and 10 other women came together to discuss the possibility of forming a women's group. These founding members felt that such a group might meet the needs of women who were sensitive about special issues, including personal anonymity, and The Winnipeg Women's Group was born.

Why start a women's group?

Fifty years ago the world was a very different place from the one it is today. There was a stigma attached to being a female alcoholic. Society felt "a woman's place was in the home," as a wife, mother and homemaker. Women were not supposed to become alcoholics; the very idea was repugnant. This attitude created a problem for many females needing our Twelve Steps. In addition, some of the women in early AA felt that the older male members were not taking them seriously at meetings. The men were polite to the women seeking sobriety, but there seemed to be a barrier to full participation in the program of recovery. Moreover, some women were also trying to recover from physical and emotional abuse; they needed time for healing before they felt comfortable enough to attend mixed AA meetings.

In those days in Manitoba, there were no treatment centers, no detox centers and no day or residential programs available to men or women. The closest thing to a detox center was a convalescent home run by Ruby Couch ("Madam Queen" to early members of the Fellowship), who let alcoholics dry out on the sofa in her living room. Because there were no residential treatment programs for men until 1958—or for women until 1966—many alcoholics stayed in psychiatric wards. Other newcomers paced their living room floors just trying to stay sober one minute at a time. They white-knuckled it—sometimes weaning themselves off alcohol slowly. Therefore, the need for the formation of a women's group was very great.

To what do we attribute our longevity?

We are a sisterhood (a fellowship of women), who care deeply about one another. We have worked hard, been lucky in many ways and have also tried to follow the guidelines suggested by our founding members 50 years ago. For example, at the first meeting of the Winnipeg Women's Group, the founders decided that our meetings would be Step discussions each Monday evening, with the last Monday of the month reserved to honor members with AA birthdays. Also, they agreed our meetings would be closed, even our birthday night, assuring the women that everyone present was an alcoholic and that they could speak freely.

As society has changed, so too has the Women's Group. During those first years, no self-respecting woman left her house without hat and gloves; public attire was more restricted. As time passed, hemlines rose and fell and rose and fell again, and trousers became more acceptable, finally giving way to blue jeans and fleece. China cups and saucers were replaced by coffee mugs in the 70s and then in the 90s by styrofoam cups. Now, herbal teas are edging out coffee.

The 70s taught us to "let it all hang out," the 80s put us in touch with our "inner child," and the 90s brought us New Age mysticism. Through it all, the program that taught us best and kept us sane and sober was still the program of Alcoholics Anonymous.

While these changes were taking place, the number of women in Alcoholics Anonymous increased substantially. In the Alcoholics Anonymous membership survey of 2001, women made up 33 percent of the Fellowship, and newcomers were coming into the program younger and younger, some while they were teenagers.

What has not changed is the need for this group. So while at various times changes in format have been suggested and implemented, our group conscience has gently nudged us to accept the old adage, "If it is not broken, don't fix it!" Consequently, we have maintained our original studies of AA's Twelve Steps and endeavored to carry the message to the woman alcoholic who still suffers. Women of all ages and backgrounds have come to this group for 50 years and found sobriety, security and serenity in the company of other AA women.

A key to the continuation of the group has been that longtime members have continued to attend on a regular basis. We have members with over 20 and 30 years at every meeting; our oldest active member has celebrated more than 40 years of sobriety. These ladies maintain that it doesn't matter how many years you are sober; you will always need this program and these Steps, and they lead us by example. Since we only meet once a week, new members are encouraged to attend other groups if possible and to take in as many meetings as they need to stay sober. As we get well we rejoin the human race.

Another factor contributing to the group's longevity has been the "meeting after the meeting," when we've sat around and talked—at the group or at a coffee shop—over gallons of coffee, sometimes till midnight. What these talks did was cement friendships and reinforce the program of Alcoholics Anonymous and its Steps. Problems were discussed and solutions offered. Older members shared their wisdom and newcomers sat on their hands to keep them from shaking, and at the edge of their seats, so they wouldn't miss anything. We learned about life and how to heal again—how to apply the Steps to our daily lives.

Today the Winnipeg Women's Group is one of 50 groups in our city. We are deeply grateful to Bill and Dr. Bob, our Higher Power, the pioneers of our group and members everywhere who have contributed to our finding the "Road of Happy Destiny" in this blessed Fellowship.

The Winnipeg Women's Group
Winnipeg, Manitoba

Women of Kiev
July 2015

The creation of the Kiev Women's group in Ukraine was a no-brainer that just kind of happened. When I lived in Kiev from 1998 to 2001, I attended a Ukrainian/Russian AA Discussion meeting. Each person spoke one language or the other, and both was OK too. One Sunday, there were some new women there. When it was their turn, one after another, three in a row, said, "I've read the Step chapters in the 'Twelve and Twelve.' Now what do I do?"

Because the discussions tended to focus on the problem with no discussion of the solution, I suggested that we read each Step out loud the way we do in Canada. The men all said dismissively, "No, no; you can read the Step at home," which of course, they probably don't. After hearing these women say, "Now what do we do?" I said, "Any woman—and that's women only, guys—who wants to do the Steps, can come to my place next Sunday. We'll do the Steps."

So that's how it started with four of us on a Sunday afternoon in my apartment. I served some sandwiches. (I didn't know until years later that when they were new, these women were hungry and didn't have money for food.) Now, they joke that they had to restrain themselves from grabbing. I didn't have a clue, because they were always dressed beautifully on the street. They may have had only one nice outfit, but that's what they saved to go out in. So they always looked lovely and well put-together.

When I lived in Kiev, we had a regular English-speaking Saturday morning AA meeting in downtown. We had just obtained a very convenient central location in an outbuilding of a church. So eventually, I got that regular meeting space in the same place for the Women's Discussion, and then other women started to come, and so it grew. They called it the Nadeeya (Hope) Group. Regular AA followed suit and started to meet in the same place. It became a sort of AA Central.

Meetings seem to have a life of their own; they thrive or wither of their own accord, most often of neglect. Over the years, there have been various soap operas with this group, like when the men kicked the Women's Discussion Group out of their space for another "regular" meeting. I was not there when that happened, but when I visited, I did tell the men a thing or two, particularly since the women had been there first. But the deed was done.

The lack of a central meeting space affected attendance, of course. But this past October, the women found another central place, and a whole bunch of the women who had not been going showed up. Apparently, the church eventually took back the little building where all the regular AA meetings were held, so even the regular meetings had to look for new space.

What happened as these women got sober was quite remarkable. One woman began renovating apartments, the only job she could get. After a few years, she started a construction company that got very busy. She explains it very simply: "I'm honest, so people hear about my work." She has a beautiful manor house in the country, unheard of in Kiev. Her son and his family live with her, and they are employed as well. All this from a woman whose husband threw her out with her 13-year-old son, so that she was living with him in one room with a mattress on the floor. I didn't know that when she was attending meetings in my apartment, looking lovely and sober.

Another woman now has a beautiful organic café in downtown Kiev. Yet another is a professor at the university. The women have all the usual problems, especially what I call the success syndrome. AA has helped them get a life, so they have successful businesses and many activities, and then they "don't have time" to go to AA meetings, which I find very scary. And so it was with one very successful businesswoman to whom I sent a 15-year congratulatory email recently. She had a friend let me know that she had started drinking after her 10-year celebration, so she was actually five years sober now. How fortunate that she had made it back to meetings and sobriety—not everyone does after a relapse. I have attended too many AA funerals of young people who "didn't have time" to go to meetings.

Nevertheless, while I was in Kiev recently, it was good to see that group of women and celebrate a couple of 14-year and one 15-year AA anniversaries. And thank goodness, the really busy one managed to get back to meetings. Good to know that AA is alive and well in Kiev, Ukraine.

Nadia S.
Ottawa, Ontario

Let Others Win the Ribbons
March 2016

I've been a lot of things in my life. I was a babysitter. I was a secretary and a nurse. I wrote commercials for radio. And I passed out free pickles in a grocery store. But most of all, I've been an alcoholic the whole time.

Before August 19, 1976, I was living in Boston and had been drinking a fifth of liquor every night for the prior 18 months. My first drink had been a fifth of Mississippi moonshine, 16 years earlier. Heavy drinking was habit. I was dealing with high-powered Boston hospital politics and finding out things I wished I hadn't.

A few years earlier, I had my first lesbian affair. There was a lot of drinking involved there too. Actually, all the time. I knew who I was. I also knew exactly how the rest of the world thought of us. In order to take care of others, I couldn't "out" myself. But then someone outed me in a very non-private way. Despite that, I carried on. That fifth-per-night helped. Or so I thought.

In between two blackouts in a Boston bar, I could no longer deny that I had no control over my drinking. Even so, it took still more drinking, as well as a suicide attempt, for me to get to AA.

What I immediately realized about AA is that it works. The core of the program is unconditional love. That was something human institutions failed consistently to provide.

I went to meetings in Boston and read the Big Book every night. I realized going to large meetings was not going to get me sober. Occupying space is one thing. Getting the message is another. So I read literature until I moved back to my home state of Arkansas in 1977.

AA in Arkansas at the time was interesting. Women sat in the back of the room, were not allowed to speak and didn't have to take any Steps beyond the Fifth Step. Women were felt to be too "delicate." And women died because of that attitude. In 1978, our first women's AA meeting was held, and more proliferated. I was there for that meeting. In 1979, our first gay and lesbian AA meeting was held. And I was there for that too.

Before I left Boston, I had spent three months in a mental health facility as a result of my suicide attempt. There I was diagnosed with manic depression and alcoholism, but my doctor didn't know much about them or what to do. It was clear to me who was in charge, and it wasn't humans.

In sobriety I have been admitted twice to a bad mental hospital. The first time I was admitted because my doctor thought I was "cured" and had discontinued my medication. The second time happened when my next doctor prescribed a medicine that resulted in psychosis. But in neither case did I drink, despite losing control over my mental abilities for weeks at a time. The doctors couldn't understand why I didn't drink. Never underestimate HP. I don't.

In 1987, I put my registered nurse license into retirement voluntarily and without any blemishes. But that immediately put my partner and me below the poverty level. Except for two days in 30 years, we have always had food, medicine and a roof over our heads. We had whatever we needed.

And we have always had sobriety. We've seen a lot of things happen that shouldn't have happened. The more we keep our relationship with HP active and working in our lives, the less we need to fear.

Today I am 70 and still live in our small Arkansas town. I grow herbs but I quit entering the county fair so others could win ribbons. Seeing the effect my herbs have on others is reward enough for me.

One of my best experiences happened when my partner, who is disabled, was asked by a nun to resuscitate a domestic violence agency in our county. My partner got the agency back up and running, even though her success came at a cost to herself. Then I continued that work for a decade, during which time over 500 women and children have been helped to safety.

We go to Hot Springs for the spring water and the Friday AA women's meeting. We go to Little Rock for the LGBT AA meeting and we attend meetings online. We get Grapevine and donate old copies here and there, including to our local prison. And in the rest of our daily 24 hours, we work the Steps.

I've never liked seeing anyone in pain. I didn't like it as a nurse, and I don't like it now. If I can do something about someone's pain, I will. Why would I not?

I knew a lot about the deadliness of alcoholism when I came into AA and I understand more today. AA was, and is, the hope for my community.

Sobriety, to me, is God's time. No longer mine. I couldn't give it to myself and I still can't keep myself sober five minutes. It's a no-brainer.

Barbara F.
Malvern, Arkansas

Oreos and a T-Shirt
October 2000

I was walking desperately along the shore of Rehoboth Beach when everything was pink and beige and the birds were feeding too busily to pay me any attention. I wanted and needed a drink. I raised my arms to the sky and bellowed, "Help me!" The birds scattered for a bit and then went back to feeding. The skies didn't open. No vision appeared.

I got back into my car, determined to find booze somewhere. In and around me, I heard, "It will be all right. Keep it simple." Now, whether I was hearing a voice from "on high" or finally losing it wasn't important. "It" was there. I heard it. The knot in my stomach unraveled. I no longer wanted a drink.

I'd been sober on a pink cloud for over two years when I moved far from my home state of New York. In 1965, small-town meetings in the Midwest could not give me what I had been used to. There were no closed discussion meetings, no Step meetings, no active females. The guy who "ran" the local group had even changed the Preamble.

Yes, I tried speaking, starting closed meetings, doing Twelfth Step work. All failed. I had nothing to give. I never doubted I was an alcoholic. I just didn't care. I was selfish, immature and full of anger and resentment. I stayed dry until 1974. Then I took pills, smoked and finally drank.

The sky didn't fall. I wasn't struck dead. But AA had spoiled my drinking. I literally went into the closet to sneak booze and anything else I could get. Everyone, and most particularly my family, "knew" I didn't drink. However, they soon learned otherwise. I embarrassed and mortified them all.

There was no Al-Anon or Alateen in the area where we lived, but the little my husband remembered from earlier Al-Anon meetings he applied, which helped our teenaged children a great deal. However, my old buddies from my original home group were 600 miles away, and so upset they couldn't help at all. My sponsor, who had also relocated, was over 2,000 miles away in another state.

Fortunately, H., a local man whom I liked and respected, got me into a "drying out" place for 10 days. Soon I met AA members from a group about an hour's drive north of our home. And since I wasn't able to drive myself, my loyal and loving husband, along with dear H., drove me to their meetings.

I maintained a very simple program. Before my head left the pillow in the morning, I took the Tenth Step, decided to make amends and forgave myself. Then, while I was getting coffee, I chanted my gratitudes. I also kept in touch with my AA friends in New York, visited them, invited them here and used the telephone a lot. I read my AA books and literature, at times just clutching the Big Book or "Twelve and Twelve" to my heart while walking around the room, as if by osmosis I could absorb all it had to say.

Then, several years ago, my son sent me a computer. By sheer determination, admitting what I didn't know and calling every 800 number to ask for help, I found online AA. A miracle!

For the past four years, I have been a member of two women's groups, which have closed meetings in "live" chat rooms. We adhere to the Traditions and Steps and pay our dues just like everyone in an F2F (face-to-face) group. We are "legal." And the women live all over the world—Japan, Korea, England, Australia, Canada and every state in the Union. I have been able to meet some of the women in person and have developed telephone relationships with half a dozen. Recently I also got to see just how loving and caring our online group had become.

About 11 months ago, a woman from Jerusalem joined our Saturday morning meeting. F., who was originally from the States, was a brilliant scientist. Then there was a car accident. She was driving. Her husband and children were killed. Was she drinking? Did she feel guilty? Of course. In her late 30s at the time, F. converted to

Catholicism and entered a convent. However, eventually she left because, as she said, "The nuns spoiled my drinking. They also caught me with the Sacristy wine." Since she and her husband had been only children, she had no other family. So after that, she lived alone and kept right on drinking.

Then F. was diagnosed with acute bone cancer. She wanted to die sober. So when a man told her about online AA and closed women's meetings, she joined the group I belonged to. A dear, loving woman in America became her online sponsor.

F. never asked, "Why me?" or wallowed in self-pity. Yes, she did tell us when she hurt, when she was lonely, and how much she thought of her children and husband who had died because she was driving drunk. She also worked the Steps with her sponsor through email, in the chat rooms and at online meetings.

A month or so ago we all received an email from F.'s online address. It was from a nurse asking for permission to print out F.'s messages, because F. was in the hospital in very bad shape. We all assented and sent posts, anecdotes, and a great deal of love and caring. Some also sent prayers. When F. came back home, she expressed her gratitude and joy for our loving and caring.

About this time, her sponsor went on a retreat with some of the women in our online groups. They had a T-shirt bearing the name of F.'s group, and everyone signed it. Her sponsor sent the shirt to F. along with a large box of Oreo cookies, which were hard for F. to get, and which, as an American, she missed.

Finally, the time came for F.'s last hospital stay in Jerusalem. The nurse, whom we all came to love, and her boyfriend, who was F.'s doctor, kept us posted. She was overwhelmed by the love sent to this sober ailing woman from all over America.

F. died the other day. Her heart had stopped a few times, and she revived. However, the last time she wasn't conscious. The doctor put the T-shirt from F.'s friends on her pillow. He then opened the box of Oreos and placed one under F.'s nose. She sniffed lightly and said weakly, "Oreos!"

Afterward, the nurse asked F.'s sponsor if she could keep the T-shirt because she felt so much love in it, and what she called "energia." Of course, now she has the T-shirt along with the knowledge that online AA is itself a miraculous "energia" and that the women in it are sober, caring, giving members of AA.

I have stayed sober for 24 years now. With the help of the tools in this program, I didn't drink through the cancer that our only daughter died from, handled my mother's hospitalization through alcoholic dementia, and have maintained a loving marriage for over 40 years. And yet I don't think I have ever worked a better program than I do now. I am secretary of a group, sponsor three women online, attend meetings, speak on the phone, and "chat"—a lot. I continue to learn more every day.

Granny M.
Ohio

Meeting at Shivaji Market
April 2012

After years of knowing I was alcoholic and my life was unmanageable, I finally became desperate and hopeless enough to land up in the rooms of AA. Sitting in those early meetings, I latched onto the Second Step—came to believe a power greater than myself would restore me to sanity. The "God business" was an issue for me. The Second Step hit me with the reality that I needed to find a palpable connection with a Higher Power in order to recover with any sort of peace. The Serenity Prayer became my lifeline once I left a meeting and went about my day. It was what got me through the early sober years when I was still working in a bar because I couldn't imagine what else I could do at that point.

I started taking yoga classes in a spiritually-based yoga institute where their teaching was "Truth is One, Paths are Many." This resonated with me, and I became willing to immerse myself in this ancient body, mind and spirit practice, which very much dovetailed with the AA program. This was the beginning of my spiritual sober journey. I felt so connected to the practice that I studied and trained to become a yoga teacher, which I completed in my third year of sobriety.

AA taught me the valuable gift of service. At 90 days, my sponsor told me it was time for me to take a commitment, so I found an opportunity to open and chair my first meeting. As an unreliable, untrustworthy alcoholic, being handed the keys to the meeting place and being trusted that I would show up in time to make the coffee and set up the room, felt huge to me. I carried that same esteem-building service into my yoga teaching and was able to take yoga classes into two women's prisons where most of the women were also substance abusers.

Marriage, children ... fast forwarding 20 years, I was offered the opportunity to travel to India, the birthplace of yoga, with a small group of people, one a dear friend who is also a sober woman. We had a list of AA meetings for the town where we would be staying for the next six weeks.

On the second day after landing in this beautiful country, we jumped into a motor-rickshaw and headed to downtown Pune to find our first AA meeting. Hair flying, we bumped through the city taking in the incredible colorful sights, sounds and scents, then got stuck in traffic as several cows moseyed across the road. The driver dropped us off at the backside of Shivaji Market, where we stepped over just-unloaded goat carcasses, trying to find the AA meeting place. Around the corner, under the portico of this very old, lovely building, stood two men. "Is there an AA meeting here?" we asked. We were very warmly greeted and welcomed with the familiar words, "You're in the right place." This group is called "The Freedom and Hope Group of Pune" and meets three times a week, offering English-speaking meetings.

Rajan took us under his wing and became our dear AA friend, cultural and historical authority and guide. He drove us to and from meetings and introduced us to his family and country in ways we would never have experienced on our own. He was a living example of love and service. The other travelers in our group had quite a different experience compared to our unique immersion into Indian culture through the loving arms of AA.

Very few women attended the meetings. We had the opportunity to be at the one-year anniversary celebration of a woman who regularly attended the "Freedom and Hope" meetings. Her husband and mother were at the meeting to join in the celebration, and her mother made delicious food for everyone as a contribution to the celebration. When the woman shared her story with the immense shame of an alcoholic woman in that culture and described her incredible struggle to get and stay sober in the very male-dominated AA community, it was an eye-opener for me. I felt tremendous gratitude and appreciation for the ease and openness of my own sobriety in the United States. This was followed by the thought, I need to help start a women's meeting here.

I had such a heart-connection with India and knew I would be back. I began talking to Rajan about a women's meeting, and he volunteered to be a behind-the-scenes person to help get things in motion there while I did what I could from the States. We had a meeting place and time, three sober women and AA literature in place for the first meeting, scheduled for July 2005. There was even an Alcoholism Awareness Public Meeting, with press attention, scheduled to take place that July.

Then a God-moment happened while I was attending the 2005 International AA Convention in Toronto. I listened as an Indian man told his story in one of the big meetings in the stadium. He said, "We have many suffering alcoholic women in our country, and they need your help! Please come and help our women get sober."

A few weeks later, the first women's AA meeting in Pune happened. I also had the pleasure of meeting Pushan, the speaker from Toronto that summer. This July, the women's meeting will celebrate its sixth anniversary, with its doors and hearts open to help the next alcoholic woman who wants to get and stay sober.

There were many times when it was questionable as to whether the few women could keep it going. One woman showed up each Sunday afternoon for two straight years—sometimes the only person sitting there for that hour—and waited for another alcoholic woman to show up. Now there is a solid, small core of faithful, sober women attending and sharing the responsibilities. Over these past five-plus years, there has been a sober woman to extend the hand of AA to the next Indian woman who finds the courage to walk through the door for help. Women continue to come from the local rehab on Sunday afternoon to learn about AA and recovery, as well as women from other countries around the world who are visiting and want the safety and warmth of a women's meeting.

I'm grateful to be a sober woman today and know the AA community is waiting to remind me that my purpose is to stay sober and to help another alcoholic, wherever I am in the world.

Deborah D.
Montclair, New Jersey

The Four of Us
August 2000

There were just four of us. Four women, treasuring our sobriety and wanting more than abstinence from alcohol alone. We attended the same AA meetings, listened to each other share and liked what we heard. But more, we got to know each other and to see the Twelve Steps working in one another's lives.

So we started getting together, just the four of us, gathering for dinner at one another's homes once a month and following dinner with a heartfelt AA meeting.

At first, two of us sponsored the other two. But even with considerable differences in our years of sobriety, no one wanted to be the group guru. Each felt the need for honest feedback to our daily concerns.

The trust gradually grew deeper, until at last we knew there was nothing we could not safely share in our after-dinner group. What actually developed was that each of us has three loving sponsors.

We have shared successes and failures, joys and sorrows, illness and health. We have shared the loss of jobs, the start of a new business, the beginning of committed new relationships, the death of a spouse and the ensuing loneliness, and a wedding. In times of stress, the woman in need could count on the understanding and empathy of the other three, just as in times of celebration, all four of us shared in the joy.

We have had vacations and holidays to share, new career opportunities to applaud and both natal and AA birthdays to celebrate. And that brings me to this very day.

Today we met in grateful celebration of a total of 106 years of AA sobriety the four of us have, and we are looking forward to 106 years and one day.

Judi C.
Carlsbad, California

The Twelve Steps

1. We admitted we were powerless over alcohol—that our lives had become unmanageable.
2. Came to believe that a Power greater than ourselves could restore us to sanity.
3. Made a decision to turn our will and our lives over to the care of God *as we understood Him.*
4. Made a searching and fearless moral inventory of ourselves.
5. Admitted to God, to ourselves, and to another human being the exact nature of our wrongs.
6. Were entirely ready to have God remove all these defects of character.
7. Humbly asked Him to remove our shortcomings.
8. Made a list of all persons we had harmed, and became willing to make amends to them all.
9. Made direct amends to such people wherever possible, except when to do so would injure them or others.
10. Continued to take personal inventory and when we were wrong promptly admitted it.
11. Sought through prayer and meditation to improve our conscious contact with God *as we understood Him,* praying only for knowledge of His will for us and the power to carry that out.
12. Having had a spiritual awakening as the result of these steps, we tried to carry this message to alcoholics, and to practice these principles in all our affairs.

The Twelve Traditions

1. Our common welfare should come first; personal recovery depends upon A.A. unity.
2. For our group purpose there is but one ultimate authority—a loving God as He may express Himself in our group conscience. Our leaders are but trusted servants; they do not govern.
3. The only requirement for A.A. membership is a desire to stop drinking.
4. Each group should be autonomous except in matters affecting other groups or A.A. as a whole.
5. Each group has but one primary purpose—to carry its message to the alcoholic who still suffers.
6. An A.A. group ought never endorse, finance or lend the A.A. name to any related facility or outside enterprise, lest problems of money, property and prestige divert us from our primary purpose.
7. Every A.A. group ought to be fully self-supporting, declining outside contributions.
8. Alcoholics Anonymous should remain forever nonprofessional, but our service centers may employ special workers.
9. A.A., as such, ought never be organized; but we may create service boards or committees directly responsible to those they serve.
10. Alcoholics Anonymous has no opinion on outside issues; hence the A.A. name ought never be drawn into public controversy.
11. Our public relations policy is based on attraction rather than promotion; we need always maintain personal anonymity at the level of press, radio and films.
12. Anonymity is the spiritual foundation of all our traditions, ever reminding us to place principles before personalities.

Alcoholics Anonymous

AA's program of recovery is fully set forth in its basic text, *Alcoholics Anonymous* (commonly known as the Big Book), now in its Fourth Edition, as well as in *Twelve Steps and Twelve Traditions, Living Sober,* and other books. Information on AA can also be found on AA's website at WWW.AA.ORG, or by writing to:

Alcoholics Anonymous
Box 459
Grand Central Station
New York, NY 10163

For local resources, check your local telephone directory under "Alcoholics Anonymous." Four pamphlets, "This is A.A.," "Is A.A. For You?," "44 Questions," and "A Newcomer Asks" are also available from AA.

AA Grapevine

AA Grapevine is AA's international monthly journal, published continuously since its first issue in June 1944. The AA pamphlet on AA Grapevine describes its scope and purpose this way: "As an integral part of Alcoholics Anonymous since 1944, the Grapevine publishes articles that reflect the full diversity of experience and thought found within the A.A. Fellowship, as does La Viña, the bimonthly Spanish-language magazine, first published in 1996. No one viewpoint or philosophy dominates their pages, and in determining content, the editorial staff relies on the principles of the Twelve Traditions."

In addition to magazines, AA Grapevine, Inc. also produces books, eBooks, audiobooks, and other items. It also offers a Grapevine Online subscription, which includes: new stories weekly, AudioGrapevine (the audio version of the magazine), Grapevine Story Archive (the entire collection of Grapevine articles), and the current issue of Grapevine and La Viña in HTML format. For more information on AA Grapevine, or to subscribe to any of these, please visit the magazine's website at WWW.AAGRAPEVINE.ORG or write to:

AA Grapevine, Inc.
475 Riverside Drive
New York, NY 10115